The Soccer Dad Chronicles

Successful Strategies for Coaching and Parenting

MISSION POINT PRESS

Published by Mission Point Press
2554 Chandler Rd.
Traverse City, MI 49696
(231) 421-9513
www.MissionPointPress.com

Design by Sarah Meiers
Cover design uses stock art from Thomas Bethge and Joanna Redesiuk

ISBN:
978-1-961302-98-3 (Softcover)
978-1-961302-97-6 (Hardcover)
Library of Congress Control Number: 2024914967

Printed in the United States of America

THE

SOCCER DAD
CHRONICLES

*Successful Strategies
for Coaching
and Parenting*

Andy Beers

MISSION POINT PRESS

To my children

Contents

Prologue

WHEN A CHILD participates in a sport, what they learn changes their life and the lives of others in unexpected ways. I was reminded of that on the day Judy and I moved our daughter Megan to college. The day was especially significant because she was our youngest child, the last of three to leave home. I did everything a good father was supposed to do. I drove while she napped in the back seat, carried her belongings to the fourth floor, moved furniture to achieve her version of feng shui, bought lunch, and chauffeured her back to the dorm. Then Judy and I hugged her, told her to use good judgment, and departed for home.

As she navigated freshman Welcome Weekend, my mind circled back to one event on drop-off day that happened while we waited to place our order for lunch. A girl ahead of Megan recognized the high school soccer logo on her T-shirt. In less than a minute, the two ascertained the identity of mutual friends and became acquainted. The positive interaction helped to ease my tension because it demonstrated that making friends would be easy for Megan. It also made me wonder to what extent the girls' soccer backgrounds played a role in their connection. They shared a common history that began before Megan was born and continued until soccer nudged them together on her first day of college. How would her life differ if we had chosen another activity?

This is the true story of my involvement as a recreational soccer coach for sixteen years. I coached the teams of all three of my children and spent a significant portion of my life sharing soccer activities with them. I frequently made potentially life-changing decisions involving my children, but I never knew how my actions would influence their futures. Those were frightening circumstances. Now, I can look back and evaluate what I did right and where I went wrong. Was it worth it? Would I do it again? I still ask those questions because there were marvelous moments when I watched my children transformed by the game of soccer, and painful incidents when I witnessed them treated unfairly or physically injured. I also influenced the lives of children who were not mine. Some embraced what I taught and became skilled, confident individuals; others were frustratingly resistant.

I had never kept a diary; however, some events were so significant that I wrote them down. I have always wanted to compile them because they tell a story my children would enjoy and from which others could learn. The story only scratches the surface of my experience. To provide a broader scope of information in a tangible way, I have also composed six summaries of tips and tricks that will guide those facing the challenges of coach development, player motivation, conflict with adults, and appropriate behavior. I hope others benefit from my hard-learned lessons, and those summary pages become dog-eared and worn from use as coaches and parents refer to them whenever they are desperate for direction or inspiring words for the team.

When I started coaching, I was ignorant about everything related to soccer. When I finished, I was a confident, knowledgeable coach, comfortable in my philosophy to make soccer fun and competitive while emphasizing mentoring over playing to win. Intuition and experience guided my approach—hindsight shows it was sound. I learned that coaching recreational sports is about much more than teaching a game. It's also an opportunity to help children overcome weaknesses, learn to win with grace, and cope effectively with losing while managing the influence of adults. Attaining that perspective was not easy, but it was a rewarding endeavor that will influence my family and me for the rest of our lives.

Chapter 1

Year 1–Baptism by Soccer

WHEN I STEP from my house on the first days of spring, my brain welcomes what my senses perceive: the sour smell of soil uncovered by melting snow, the raucous squabbles of birds at a feeder, the gentle warmth of the sun on my face, and the intense green of newly emerged leaves. It's perfect and peaceful for a few moments, but then my brain connects the sensations of the present with the memories of my past, and I crave one more thing—the thud of a foot on a soccer ball.

When I was growing up, I never played soccer, I never watched soccer, and I never wanted to be a soccer coach. Coaching soccer was thrust upon me when Judy and I decided that a sport involving running and balls would be good for our six-year-old son. Owen was a constantly moving, busy child. We tried tee-ball, but the pace was too slow for him. He spent his time on the field kicking up dust clouds and grinding holes into the ground by spinning in his kid-sized baseball cleats. He was a natural but didn't love the game and was a little bored, so we continued our search.

The first time we suggested soccer, he was five years old. Owen was reluctant because he lacked experience with the game. We encouraged him, but he was unwilling, so we relented and waited. A year later, we suggested soccer again. The exchange was one of our first genuinely adult conversations. The opportunity came as we sat at our kitchen table on a lazy Saturday morning. Judy did most of the talking and adopted a playful, humorous mood like moms do when they state something ridiculously obvious.

"I think you will like it," she said. "There will be lots of running, which you like to do, and lots of balls. You will be playing with your friends, which is also something you enjoy."

Owen listened as Judy continued, "There will be practices after school during the week and games in parks around town on Saturdays. And if you don't like it, you can quit. We want you to have a good time."

I chimed in with a supportive nod and, "Yup," but it was unnecessary. That last part had sealed the deal. It was a no-risk offer of something that sounded fun. Owen thought for a minute, then said, "Okay." That was the beginning of our family soccer experience. I didn't know it, but I had just become a soccer coach.

I was thirty-six years old, and we lived in a university town where soccer was well organized. Thousands of kids played soccer on fields surrounded by cheering parents every weekend. The local soccer club oversaw that activity. It distributed registration forms, collected money, processed registration forms, assigned players to teams, painted fields, and, if no one volunteered, randomly picked a parent to be a coach and get things started. That "coach's" job was to contact each player and arrange the first practice. I unknowingly dodged that bullet. Instead, Kathy was selected, and she called us to organize things.

A few days later, we met at a local school playground. Kathy introduced herself to our group and explained that she was the designated coach but lacked firsthand soccer knowledge. She wanted help. Her statement confused Judy and me because her title and the bag of equipment she possessed bolstered her authority. We assumed she had the experience to warrant the appointment. To her credit, Kathy came to practice with some activities and a sign-up sheet for the postgame treat. Those things only reinforced our confusion. We thought she was the coach and let her take the lead because we did not want to overstep.

Under Coach Kathy's direction, we adopted a communal approach to soccer, but as practice progressed, I realized that none of the parents knew how to teach the game—though some had played a little. Like me, they showed up because they thought soccer was the right thing to do for their kids, but without experience, coaching soccer was challenging.

I grew up in a midwestern rural community at a time when few people played soccer. Instead, I played what Americans called football and participated in it during grade school and high school. I was not a great player, but my football coaches taught me a few fundamental things that are almost universal in athletics: step and kick, stay on your toes, bend your knees to lower your center of gravity so you can move quickly, and keep your head up so you can see your opponent. Armed with those basics, anyone can coach six-year-old soccer players. Since I didn't know much about soccer, I defaulted to that skill set on the first day. I emphasized good form, and things worked out. Players improved, and I began thinking about the game.

The nine boys on our team were all first-time players except one named Nathan. He was a friend of Owen's from school. Judy and I were glad that Owen knew at least one kid on the team, but our relief was short-lived. While we practiced, Judy chatted with Nathan's mom. She told Judy that because his skill level was more advanced than the rest of the team, she would inquire if he could be moved up one age level—there must have been a spot for him elsewhere because Nathan did not return.

BY THE SECOND practice, I realized I had a knack for diagnosing why a player struggled with a particular skill and was good at suggesting how to improve. Unfortunately, other parents lacked that ability, and I wondered why they didn't help appropriately. In general, parents either did nothing or tried to teach skills that were too advanced. They were teaching what they knew, but it was not what needed to be taught.

One parent, a tie-dyed dad, stood out. He had many beautiful, tie-dyed T-shirts but terrible teaching instincts. His idea of a productive drill was to challenge a player, take their ball, and then use his body to shield them from it. He defeated every player but only succeeded in teaching them how it felt to be dominated by a grown man with soccer experience and the ability to block them from the ball using a technique that put his butt in their face. I tried to redirect his actions by briefly stepping in and conferring, "Don't take the ball from them. Challenge and make them move the ball around you."

He didn't say a word and either misunderstood or disagreed because he resumed his butt-shielding activity. That was my first lesson: Not all people are good coaches. His heart was in the right place, but he lacked the experience and judgment to do the right thing. Fortunately, soccer drills don't last forever, and we moved on to the next activity—a scrimmage.

Kids participate in soccer because they want to play, so it made sense to our group of parent coaches to end practices with a scrimmage. But we could have done much more. A good soccer practice has four elements: a warmup, an introduction to a skill, a drill that highlights the skill, and a game that reinforces use of the skill. Unfortunately, our group of novice coaches was unaware of the convention. Our practices started with step two, which usually emphasized dribbling and shooting, then went straight to step four. Step four was simple: divide the team into two squads and scrimmage. That was when I first heard Kathy shout three words that I came to regard as the mark of a novice coach.

One squad dominated the scrimmage while the other struggled, managing only to chase the player with the ball. The weaker team looked tired and ready to go home. Frustrated with what she perceived as a lack of enthusiasm, Coach Kathy shouted, "Get the ball." She urged the players on, but her voice sounded screechy and a little angry. Nothing changed; no player responded. A minute passed, and she shouted again—still nothing.

She was right. The weaker team needed to change their play, but they didn't know what to do, and telling them to "get the ball" did not relay helpful information. I knew something was wrong with what she was doing, especially because she seemed to be yelling at players out of frustration, but I couldn't put my finger on why it was wrong and how to fix it. That was the challenge of being an inexperienced coach—I didn't know what else to do. "Getting the ball" sounded simple, but it wasn't. Coach Kathy needed to break down the process and teach players a skill to help them achieve what she wanted.

If I were to teach an adult to solve a calculus problem, I would not give them a pencil and paper and shout, "Solve the problem." Instead, I would introduce them to new mathematic techniques and instruct them to use their existing algebra and thinking skills to find a solution. Similarly, "getting the ball" requires new tactics that build on existing athletic ability. Those skills are simple on their own. Each step is relatively easy and logical, but none of us parents knew the process. We were all uninformed, so we shouted, worked on skills, and scrimmaged in preparation for our first game.

The team was coming together. We had some players, including Owen, with natural abilities and some who could have been more enthusiastic. It seemed like an acceptable mix, and we thought we were ready for the first game. We looked forward to game day on Saturday.

Chapter 2

First Game, First Great Moment

OWEN AND I both felt uneasy about our first game. Although we spent a couple of weeks practicing soccer, neither of us had ever played a game, and we were uncomfortable not knowing what to expect. I was thinking about coaching-related things like how to kick off or interact with referees. Owen was worried about playing well and avoiding embarrassment. On game day, we ate breakfast, then Owen put on his uniform, and we warmed up for a while in the backyard. As game time drew near, Judy and I loaded Owen and his little brother, Wade, into the van and headed to the park.

We arrived a few minutes early so Owen and I could watch the end of the game played before ours. It was a cool but sunny September morning. We arrived at a field surrounded by shouting parents and populated by six players from each team. Our players were small, and so was everything else. The pitch was about forty feet wide by sixty feet long; the goals were about four feet tall by six feet wide. The convention was that teams occupied opposite sides of the field, and parents stayed with the teams. A single referee regulated the game with the help of one parent from each sideline to act as a side judge when the ball went out of bounds. Games comprised four ten-minute quarters with a ten-minute break at halftime. Lastly, there were no goalkeepers for our age group. Every player was supposed to be actively involved in the game. However, some always wanted to stand in the goal and defend it regardless of where the ball was.

Parenting is a process bursting with first-time experiences. Most adults do not spontaneously decide to attend a child's soccer game, even if they are unusually curious. I was no different from most. Because I never played soccer and lacked an enthusiastic niece or nephew who invited me to one of their games, I needed to learn quickly to succeed as a first-time coach. I felt nervous as I watched because some players were much better than ours, but I grew more confident as I learned how games progressed. Finally, the referee gave his whistle three long blasts, signifying the end of the game. The two teams lined up at midfield, and players and coaches shook hands. Then, the event was over. Players and siblings ran everywhere while one group of parents started to depart so the next set of parents could move in. Coach Kathy directed our players to a spot on the sideline near midfield, and parents arranged their blankets or folding chairs in a row behind the team.

The day's first challenge was that the grass was wet with dew, an inconvenience for those who had neglected to bring something to sit on or were sensitive to clammy toes. The second challenge, the other team, was a more significant concern because they were better prepared and more capable than us. The first half was a blur as our inexperienced players and coaches struggled. Kathy mostly let the team play because she didn't know what else to do. When the referee signaled halftime, we trailed and regrouped as best we could. Once again, the other team was better prepared with a snack of oranges; we managed with water and Gatorade.

During the second half, Kathy became frustrated and often shouted at players to "Get the ball." Her instructions went unheeded. Every parent was yelling. I doubt any player could perceive helpful information through the noise. Ultimately, we did not win, but the game was competitive.

For me, the day's highlight came at the game's end. The final whistle blew, and the two teams headed to the middle of the field to shake hands. I did not go because I was just a helper parent; Kathy was the coach. As I watched, an incredible feeling of relief came over me. We had made it through our first game, and Owen had done well. With a sense of accomplishment, I felt the urge to hug and congratulate him, so I started to walk out onto the field. He was halfway back from the handshake when he saw me. We made eye contact, and he must have read my mind. He broke into a run, carving out an arcing path across the field before leaping into my arms. It was a solid chest bump that transformed into a hug and a Disney moment. He wrapped his arms around my neck and clung to me with his sweaty little body, like a ball of muscle and energy, his scratchy soccer cleats against my legs. I hugged him back. The moment didn't last long. Then he was gone, passing it on to Judy and Wade. The combination of relief and a sense of accomplishment, coupled with my child's gratitude, made that moment one of the best of my life.

Chapter 3

Hooked for Life

IT WOULD BE an overstatement to say that Owen's hug hit me like a lightning bolt, but it did hook me deeply. That hug and the surge of dopamine it produced in my brain convinced me that soccer was good for him. His reaction persuaded me that he had enjoyed the experience and that positive things could be achieved regardless of whether a game was won or lost. He had a great time; I saw it in his eyes and behavior.

Why he responded the way he did was unclear to me. It wasn't scoring a goal or attaining a tremendous victory—neither of those things happened. It was something else that had to do with his brain perceiving a reward for intangible properties like overcoming a novel challenge or working together to achieve a common goal. Intangibles were not in my thoughts that day after our first game, and they wouldn't occur to me for years. My decisions were made in the blind as I forged ahead without experience, doing what I thought was right.

The other thing Owen's hug did was put me on a collision course with other soccer participants, especially coaches, because we were motivated by different interests. I was participating to parent my child; some other soccer dads and moms were there to lead their child's team to victory. They dreamed of the day when they could field eleven players on the big field, win it all, throw up their hands in triumph, and get drenched by the contents of a Gatorade bucket. That was not my dream. I hoped for wins but was motivated more by physical fitness, fair play, teamwork, and fun.

Those contrasting philosophies pitted us against each other and produced conflict that often confronted me before I could respond effectively. Solving a problem while still learning the game's rules was difficult. To become an effective coach, I had to live the experience while investing effort to build a foundation of knowledge and, perhaps, wisdom. Amid that struggle, children were looking to me for guidance and leadership. That was a sobering responsibility, but there was a silver lining: it was soccer for six-year-olds. How hard could it be?

Chapter 4

Toilet Paper and Vomit

THERE WAS MUCH to do the following week. Coach Kathy took the lead but was running out of ideas. On the other hand, I had a list of weaknesses that needed attention based on our performance in the game. One of them was our kickoff.

Soccer kickoffs are confusing to players and parents accustomed to playing American football. In American football, opponents kick off to the other team; in soccer, the objective is to kick off and keep possession. That can be accomplished in various ways; unfortunately, no one on our team had thought about teaching them. It was apparent to me that walking up to the center line and starting the game by blasting the ball to our opponent made no sense because they came right back at us. So, I studied and went to practice with a roll of toilet paper and a lecture in my head about maintaining possession.

There was no lined field at the schoolyard where we practiced. We made do by demarcating an area using cones, but lines would have been a better tool for providing reference points for our young players. Without lines, it was difficult for players to get a feel for the size of the field and where they should be relative to other teammates. So, when we finished our dribbling and shooting drills, and Kathy looked to me for suggestions of what we should do next, I whipped out my toilet paper and said, "I think we should practice kickoffs."

Kathy stared at me in a way that expressed confusion and concern, probably because toilet paper has a specific purpose. Before she could ask an awkward question, I used it to make a centerline on our imaginary field. Then I instructed half our team to prepare for kickoff by toeing the centerline (which they did because they could see it) and arranged the remaining players in opposition. I explained that instead of kicking the ball to the other team, we would pass it sideways to one of our players so they could receive it and dribble toward the goal. That said, I picked a player to kick and got out of the way. The outcome was predictable: the first player blasted the ball straight ahead to the other team, like always. I stepped in and halted play. "Try it again," I said as I repositioned players. A second chance was all it took. The kicker passed the ball across the field toward his teammate. The defending team knew our plan, so they jumped the ball and won it, but the seed of the concept was planted in those six-year-old brains. The toilet paper lasted long enough to give each team a couple of tries, and then we finished the day with a scrimmage.

That weekend, we blasted the ball to the other team on kickoffs, but we had orange slices at halftime, so we were on a roll. Shouting "get the ball" still wasn't working, and we didn't win, but our first-time players were becoming more comfortable and aggressive. Owen seemed to be having fun. "Two games down, six to go. Just get through it," Judy and I told each other.

BY THE FOURTH week of practice, parent participation dwindled. That was okay because we settled into a routine. Our striking had improved dramatically from the first practice. "Step and kick," I told players, and with each repetition, their kicks became crisper. All aspects of our game were improving, but unlike many opponents, we didn't have a star player. That was the random factor in coaching a recreational soccer team. Teams were stuck with assigned players, and sometimes, no matter how hard they worked, they didn't have the natural ability to go toe-to-toe with others. As coaches faced with that reality, all we could do was try to make soccer fun while teaching the fundamentals of dribbling, passing, and shooting.

It didn't seem right that our star, Nathan, left the team because his parents didn't think our group was competitive enough. They saw struggling coaches and weak players and intervened on their son's behalf. Their actions disrupted the parity between teams established by the Soccer Club's semi-random player assignment process, and we were the victims of their decision. I wondered how Nathan might have responded if his parents viewed the situation as a teaching moment and told him, "You have a chance to lead this team. Lead by example. Don't flaunt your ability. Teach them what you know and help them get better." Nathan was a nice boy and a good athlete. If he had been given the proper encouragement and stayed with our team, he could have learned leadership as well as how to kick a soccer ball.

Our game that week became etched in my memory

because of one thing—chunky vomit. The event started well. Our team was focused and competitive, but by halftime, we trailed our opponent by a goal. As players came off the field, they grabbed a drink and looked for orange slices. Unfortunately, there were none because someone forgot their responsibility. There was a long, awkward pause as we all stared across the field at the other team devouring their energy-rich delicacy. The tie-dyed family had the end-of-the-game treat that week. It was a spectacularly large stainless-steel bowl filled with a great variety of granola bars and cookies—more than enough for every player. Not wanting to disappoint, they offered up the bowl. The gesture seemed like a bad idea to me because the bowl held more than required for a halftime snack, but Kathy was the coach.

When the bowl hit the ground, it was like hungry lions on a dead zebra. The sound of ripping wrappers and ravenous chewing shattered the peaceful halftime break. The tie-dyed player must have been coveting the treats for days because he stood over the bowl and stuffed in one after another. Ten minutes were enough for the carnage to subside and our eight boys to get their fill. Then the referee called us back to the field. The team played well at first. Our opponent pressured hard, but we fought off the attacks. Players were working and doing a lot of running, but their circulatory systems could not simultaneously supply the needs of their legs and digestive tracts. It took about six minutes for the tie-dyed kid's stomach to reject its contents. He was near our sideline when he suddenly stopped running and started coughing. It was an ugly cough, the kind that attracts a parent's attention. His back was to me, but I saw his body hunched over, silhouetted against the morning sun as he began to hurl chunky granola.

The ref stopped the game and signaled to our sideline for help. Parents and Coach Kathy converged on the afflicted player cautiously, careful not to get too close. I was confused and greatly concerned. Then as the second kid started to heave in a less spectacular fashion, I realized what was happening. All that running on a full stomach was not a good combination.

Fortunately, only three players suffered that day because of bad parental judgment, and Owen was not one of them. There was no penalty for delay-of-game due to chain-reaction barfing. The referee let the clock run while the pukefest proceeded, so the second half went fast. We didn't win. Nobody cared. We were just glad that it was over.

The rest of the season was a blur of practices and games. By the end of October, it was over. We managed to win two games, and our players improved. Owen was addicted and loved soccer. He had a knack for dribbling the ball closely in a crowd and was becoming the standout player on our team. A new soccer ball would be on his Christmas list, and more coaching was in my future.

Andy's Advice ... for First-Time Coaches and Soccer Parents

The environment surrounding first-time soccer participants is filled with uncertainty. Players and coaches are unsure how to participate, and inexperienced parents with strong emotional ties to their children don't know how to behave during physical soccer games. Follow the lead of individuals with more experience.

For coaches:

1. **Don't fear coaching** because you lack knowledge or experience if you are willing to learn the game.
2. **Be positive.** Build on what players do well and emphasize the importance of having fun.
3. **Be flexible and patient.** Teaching soccer is a process, and the pace of learning varies for each player.
4. **Prepare.** Carry a pocket notebook to script practices and games. Seek the advice of a mentor or someone with soccer experience. Observe other coaches.
5. **Be creative.** Kids who dislike soccer drills will enthusiastically dribble a ball for the opportunity to destroy an alien in the goal.

For parents:

1. **Be a committed parent.** Help your player learn responsibility by reminding them to organize their equipment, arrive on time for practices and games, tie their shoes, and label their water bottle.
2. **Be positive and patient.** Players and coaches are doing their best. Give them time to find their rhythm.
3. **Befriend the coach and offer to help.** First-time coaches have much in common with first-time soccer parents.
4. **Prepare.** Read a book or other resources for first-time soccer parents. Learn the game.
5. **Temper your urge to protect your child.** Be tolerant and rational during games.

Chapter 5

Off-Season Activities

THE WEATHER DURING our winter off-season was relatively mild, with many sunny, dry days. Owen often played soccer at school during recess with a new friend, Jackson, whose family had temporarily relocated to the area. The two became fast friends and played together every day.

Judy and I spent the time working and parenting. I was a research scientist at the university, and Judy was a psychologist. My job was a "soft-money" position, meaning I was self-funded. I obtained my income by writing proposals and conducting field and laboratory research. It was a precarious way to earn a living, made easier because I worked in a laboratory with similarly funded researchers, and we helped each other succeed.

Some aspects of my job were exciting. I had investigations in remote parts of the western United States and worked in spectacular locations for a few weeks every year. Fieldwork made my job more interesting, but there was an unfortunate tendency for one of our sons to get sick whenever I left town on a trip. When that happened, Judy had to cancel her clients and reschedule so she could stay home with a sick child. Most of her patients were good-natured about the inconvenience.

Still, it seemed unfair that she had to sacrifice her work under those circumstances.

As winter turned to spring, our family started to think about soccer again. I attended a clinic for beginner coaches presented by the Soccer Club. It was taught by an older coach who was very laid back about playing soccer. His demeanor and how he explained the game de-emphasized winning and highlighted having fun in a positive environment. He mentioned that parents often get in the way of that philosophy and said that deep down, he wished they would drop their kids off at games and stay away until it was all over. As a parent, I was confused by his statement; it was counterintuitive, but I made a mental note. He also encouraged coaches not to pay attention to the score and advised that if a player asks about it, tell them we didn't keep score. He had more experience than I, and his justification made sense to me. The idea of emphasizing fun rather than the score appealed because that is what I wanted Owen to get from the experience—fun.

I didn't have dreams of him becoming an Olympic athlete who needed to train his entire life to achieve a pinnacle of success. That seemed unrealistic because it wasn't in his family history or our temporal and fiscal budgets. I wanted a positive, fun experience that made him physically fit and provided an opportunity to experience success as part of a team. I knew he would not win all of his games, and I had no answer for the self-imposed question, "If winning is all a player cares about, what do they take away from a loss?" Consequently, I embraced my instructor's philosophy of de-emphasizing the score and forged ahead without knowing the answers to all the questions about how to be a successful soccer coach.

JUDY AND I were getting to know the ins and outs of recreational soccer. While I was preparing for another coaching
experience, Judy played the registration game. Thousands of
kids played soccer in our city. Parents lined up at the soccer
office on the first registration day because they had to act fast
to get their players on the neighborhood team. There was a lot
of turnover on teams in Owen's age group, and it was likely
that he would be assigned a new one. We wanted him to join
our local team so he could play with his school friends. Judy
registered early to increase the chances that we got what we
wanted. The plan worked. When we showed up for the first
practice in April, Jackson and several of Owen's other friends
were there.

Chapter 6

Teamwork Emerges

THE SPRING SEASON was as different as night and day from our previous experience. Judy was acquainted with Cori, one of the moms on the team. She had played soccer in high school and was willing to coach. I volunteered to help. Cori hit the ground running at the first practice with a sign-up sheet for halftime oranges and postgame snacks. Best of all, our assigned practice locality included a lined soccer field!

Cori had an excellent demeanor. She was calm, with an upbeat coaching style. Under her tutelage, we embraced a more standard soccer model where she warmed up the team, introduced a skill, reinforced it with a drill, and then finished practice with a scrimmage. We worked on dribbling, passing, throw-ins, and spreading out. Spreading out was difficult for six-year-old players to comprehend. Their brains told them that the best way to get the ball was to run toward it regardless of whether a teammate or opponent had possession. For them, the idea of facilitating a pass by running away from a teammate who had the ball was counterintuitive. The coach who taught my soccer clinic called it bunch ball. Like dogs with the same favorite toy, our players wanted to run to the ball and compete for it. Cori and I tried to teach them that the ball would come to them if they could get open. It was one of those concepts that we introduced on many occasions. Using words to encourage players to spread out wasn't productive. It didn't matter how often we demonstrated, explained, or justified the concept; we couldn't break the tendency to run to the ball. It occurred to me that we needed to retrain their brains, so with Cori's permission, I emphasized the skill when we practiced throw-ins.

"When the ball goes off the field, there is usually a bunch of players around it. When the throw is ours, you must spread out so your teammate can get the ball to you. We are going to practice spreading out," I explained. "First, we need to bunch up," I said as I picked up a ball and held it to my chest. Then I shouted, "Bunch!" and waited for the team to encircle me. They hesitated but gradually formed a giggling pod.

I raised the ball over my head as if I was going to throw it onto the field and shouted, "Spread!" Players tentatively fanned out around me, and I threw the ball to one who was farthest away. Instantly, everyone seemed to understand what was necessary to receive the ball. "Bunch!" The pod formed again. "Spread!" Players quickly dispersed farther and more enthusiastically. With many of them in good positions, I rewarded one with the ball. Then I handed the ball to one of Owen's teammates, and we practiced a few more times. The drill was simple, fun, and evoked competition between players, but the best thing was that it ingrained a response to the "spread" command. Our players lacked situational awareness to recognize when to spread out, but after the drill, they knew how to respond to the call. Still, weeks went by before anyone embraced the concept. When the breakthrough came, it was remarkable, and Owen and Jackson opened the floodgates.

A CORNER KICK is how gameplay is restarted when a ball, last touched by a defender, goes off the field over the end line without a goal being scored. It is awarded to the attacking team, and the kick is taken from the corner nearest where the ball left the field. Ideally, a corner kick goes directly into the goal or to a teammate, but we were playing bunch ball, which meant that the ball encountered a mob almost as soon as it entered the field of play. The innovation came during a game when Owen and Jackson, who had been soccer buddies all winter, figured out that a corner kick was a great opportunity to spread out and play together.

As Jackson lined up to take a corner kick, players from both teams bunched in front of him. Owen was on the edge of the mob, frustrated that he couldn't get Jackson's attention. In desperation, he stepped away from the group into the surrounding open space. His movement immediately caught Jackson's eye, and their training took over. As Jackson shifted his feet to kick the ball to his friend, Owen had a moment of greater insight. He saw that the goal was undefended and signaled to Jackson as he ran to it. Jackson understood the message, and instead of kicking the ball to the pod of players clustered around him, he sent a rolling line drive in Owen's direction. The ball lost momentum as it traveled and was barely moving when it reached its intended target. Owen handled it efficiently, trapped it, then tapped it in.

Cheers erupted from the parents while Owen and Jackson high-fived each other and the rest of the team. I was elated; it was a clever play. The most impressive thing about it was the teamwork. I looked at Judy and said, "Wow, where did that come from?" She laughed and shook her head.

Meanwhile, the game continued. About three minutes later, both teams found themselves in the same situation. As Jackson prepared to take the corner kick and Owen lined up in front of the undefended goal, coaches and parents from the other team desperately shouted in vain for someone to cover Owen, but their players were bunched up and focused on the ball. Jackson kicked another line drive to Owen, who knocked it in. It was too easy and too good to last. A few minutes later, it was *déjà vu* all over again, but the other team had gotten the message. Two defenders sandwiched Owen between them, Jackson's kick was not as good, and his pass was intercepted. The breakthrough tipped the score in our favor. More importantly, our players began to understand the advantages of spreading out.

THAT SPRING, OWEN emerged as an exceptional dribbler. Most soccer players have two feet, but not all can dribble a ball equally well with both. Owen was fortunate to be one of the few who could. He had a grandma and grandpa who were left-handed. Those genes gave him an atypical set of abilities: he threw a ball with his right hand but batted a ball and wrote with his left. When he kicked a ball, he had nearly equal ability with both feet, a condition known as "two-footed." The ability gave him an ease with the ball that most players did not have. He was especially good in a crowd. I witnessed his ability on an occasion when I was arms-length from him. I was on the sideline, but so close to the action I could smell sweat and hear breathing as four players battled in a bunch-ball stalemate. They kicked and stabbed at the ball like a confused octopus. Seconds ticked by, and the stalemate continued long enough for Owen to join. He ran to the group, picked a gap between two players, and raised his arms like the V on a snowplow. Then he drove through the pile. Players flew like characters in a Loony Tunes cartoon, and Owen emerged with the ball and was on the run.

When things went well, the soccer season flew by. We won about half of our games and were competitive in all. There was a feeling of accomplishment because we jelled as a team, Owen became a standout dribbler, and I began to understand my role. I was comfortable with the way games were played and knew what referees expected. Despite my inexperience with soccer, I was confident that my athletic knowledge was adequate to improve the skills and techniques of our young players. I successfully led practices in Cori's absence on several occasions, utilizing her coaching style. The whole experience differed from the previous undertaking, which had felt like a constant struggle. The new routine was one of organized player development, improvement, and fun.

By Memorial Day, the season was over; two weeks later, school was out. Unfortunately, our team did not stay together. Jackson and his family moved away. Despite Judy's skill at the registration game, Owen was assigned to a different group and a new coach for the upcoming fall season.

Chapter 7

Year 2–Handsome Dan

COACH DAN WAS a handsome guy. He was young and fit, with a great smile and a friendly demeanor. Every mom on the team probably had the hots for him. Luckily, he was married and had a son on Owen's new soccer team. Dan grew up playing rec soccer and continued playing in the competitive high school league. That experience made him a total package because, to top it all off, he was well-organized and a terrific coach. Those characteristics were my dream come true, and I volunteered to help.

The greatest thing about Dan was how easygoing he was. That quality got my attention during our second practice when one player was uncomfortable participating. Dan had introduced a new skill, and as he began rotating players through the drill, Tyler hesitated. The skill was relatively easy. Most players jumped right in and were having fun, but Tyler was the smallest player on the team, timid and quiet. He probably felt anxious about his teammates' competitiveness, or maybe he was hungry or tired.

When it was his turn, Tyler was on the verge of tears. He approached Dan and said, "I don't want to play."

Without hesitation, Dan took on the demeanor of a concerned dad, knelt, and asked, "Are you okay?"

"Yes, I just don't want to play," Tyler confirmed.

Dan smiled and said, "Okay, no problem; you can step to the side for a few minutes until you are ready to return."

I watched Tyler's demeanor go from trepidation to total relief in two seconds. By saying, "Okay," Dan defused the situation and gave the young player the power to make a decision—one he did not think would be his. Dan's solution diminished Tyler's anxiety, and I could see the mental chain of events play out on his face. He went from feeling intimidated to relieved and then confused when he realized that he had voluntarily taken himself out of a fun drill and had to watch from the sideline. It took about ten seconds for a smiling Tyler to return and announce, "I'm ready to play."

As I watched the interaction unfold, I was surprised by how Dan's approach differed from what I would have done. My impulse was to encourage Tyler to participate by instilling confidence and being optimistic. I would have said, "Don't worry, give it a try." I doubt my method would have worked because practice would have been disrupted when Tyler burst into tears. Good coaches succeed by borrowing tricks from other coaches. Defusing an emotional situation by giving a player what they wanted was a tool I frequently used for the next fourteen years.

WHILE I LEARNED all I could from Dan, Owen acquainted himself with his teammates. They were all from the same neighborhood and knew each other. Owen's skill with the soccer ball quickly solidified his standing with the group. Player for player, we were better than average, and although some players would come and go, we had several at our core.

First, there was Owen, a great dribbler and solid defender. Second, Dan's son Cody, like his father, was fast and a good shot. He loved to play and was willing to share the ball with teammates, which improved our passing game. Another kid, Drew, was not fast but was big and territorial, characteristics that made him a good defender. Drew was also a master of bodily functions. He honed his craft routinely during warm-up when the team was arranged in a circle. Not one to waste a captive audience, he farted through the butterfly stretch, grabbed a quick drink of water, and belched the alphabet. It was humorous and offensive. Drew's behavior caught me off guard. Some parents would not have allowed it, but Dan and I did because Drew's sense of humor brought something unique to our team and created an opportunity to build trust with players by showing them they were free to act like boys. We also didn't object because Drew was a multitasker who could fart *and* stretch simultaneously, and we felt foolish trying to scold him while laughing uncontrollably.

Drew's next-door neighbor and best friend was Darren. Darren was fast but not always attentive. Picking dandelions or catching a butterfly during a game was not beyond him. His saving grace was his friendship with Drew because, despite their weaknesses, they had each other's back and played well together.

Tyler, the hesitant first-time player, was not aggressive but always came to practice and worked to improve. He was the kind of player I worried about on a soccer field because he was so little. The remarkable thing about him was that although he may have lacked the skill to stop a more aggressive player, he was never afraid to try.

Helping a small, seven-year-old boy find the confidence to physically challenge a larger, faster opponent was one of the best things we did as coaches. From a player's standpoint, that confidence came from the expectation that the game's rules provided protection. It also came from knowing that each player was responsible for fulfilling an obligation to their teammates. Dan and I reinforced that attitude with something simple—equal playing time. That idea was emphasized at my first soccer clinic, where the instructor advised, "Don't emphasize the score. Expose players to every position and give them equal time on the field." I did not realize how important those things were when I applied the philosophy. I did it because that is what the Soccer League recommended, and it seemed fair to me. It wasn't until years later, when I introduced the expectation of equal playing time to a squad that had never experienced it, that I learned how it made a team stronger by giving players responsibility.

EVERY SEASON, DAN guided our team through one of the most important events a team could confront—choosing a name. It was a democratic process that began with a huddle of boys brainstorming ideas. They enthusiastically shouted out a progression of candidates inspired by familiar professional teams whose names were transformed into chimeras with superpowers, "Rockies, Greyhounds, Speed Dogs, Rocket Dogs," until a consensus of several viable options emerged.

Then Dan organized a show of hands to narrow the field from three to two to one. Bullet Dogs was the first.

The Bullet Dog season went fast. We had determined players and the speed to take the attack to other teams. Owen loved it—almost too much. After dinner, he frequently appeared with a soccer ball and begged me to go out to the cul-de-sac and kick. After a long day, it was sometimes difficult to get out of my chair and go to the street to punt a ball, but it was always rewarding to participate in soccer's version of a game of catch between father and son as we shared some time.

Chapter 8

Megan Sees Her Shadow

THE FOLLOWING SPRING, our core players stayed together on the team, and we were fortunate to gain one more kid from the neighborhood, Kyle, who was quick and had moves. Kyle amped up our attack and made my job as coach easy. The season flew by, and we wrapped up a winning season the week before Memorial Day. With the distraction of soccer behind me, I settled in at work to get some things done.

One morning in late June, I worked alone in my office. The space where I worked was designed around a central laboratory with offices around the perimeter. Mine was a room near the back of the lab. As I sat at my desk grinding away on a report, I heard the squeak of hinges on the main entrance door followed by the staccato tip-tap of women's shoes on the floor. At first, I ignored the sounds, but as the footsteps approached my door, they took on a familiar tone. I turned to find my smiling wife knocking at the open door.

A visit from her was unusual, so I was surprised but glad for the distraction. "Hi, what's going on?" I said. She smiled and handed me a small brown paper lunch bag with the top folded neatly shut. Confused, I opened the bag and pulled out a pink 3x5 note card. As I read the words on the card, I blushed as a wave of surprised emotion surged—we were having a baby. The card said we should expect delivery in February. The estimate was correct: like a little groundhog, our daughter Megan saw her shadow for the first time on February 2 at 8:03 in the morning.

She could kick from the day she was born. There was more soccer coaching in my future.

Chapter 9

Year 3–Increasing Role

COACH DAN EARNED his living managing construction crews. During the first year of our collective experience, he and I successfully juggled jobs and volunteer coaching, but Dan must have been as good at managing adult tradespeople as he was at teaching seven-year-olds soccer because he grew busier as time went on. He could only manage one weekly practice by our second fall soccer season. Consequently, on Tuesdays, Dan and I introduced new soccer skills; on Thursdays, I alone reinforced them. I adopted Dan's coaching style to avoid confusion and because I didn't know any other way. The system worked well. The boys were comfortable with us but still respected us. We never had an attendance problem at practices or games, and we won frequently enough that players were having a good time. All those things made coaching easier, and I gained confidence.

I was fortunate. The team embraced me as one of their own. I never intended to become one of the boys, but an ease developed between us. That relationship was rewarding and especially fun because young boys laugh often, and I was allowed to participate.

One sweltering Thursday afternoon at the end of practice.

Everyone was hot and tired as we crossed the field to our bikes. Shade trees offered welcome relief from the sun, so we paused to hang out and cool off before the ride home. A minute or two elapsed, then Drew got the idea to empty his water bottle over his head. His action triggered a burst of activity as others followed his example. Darren, who always wore artfully styled cornrows and braids ornamented with colorful beads, was the last to join in. Determined not to be left out, he wore a gleam in his eye as he retrieved an aluminum water bottle from his bike and opened it. He raised the bottle over his head and paused, heightening everyone's anticipation, then tipped it upside down. His teammates and I expected a flood of icy water. Instead, warm, viscous milk sluggishly glugged from the bottle. It flooded over his beautiful braids and then down his back and forehead. There were no lumps, but I wondered how many days that milk had been in the uninsulated container. The team erupted in disgusted groans and laughter. Darren looked surprised and then giggled at his mistake.

Several boys comically fell to the ground at the hilarious event, but it wasn't over. As we loitered in the schoolyard, reliving what happened, Darren's mom appeared. She worried when he didn't come home after practice and walked over to check on him. Without a clue of what transpired, but with the innate instinct that only a mother possesses, she reached out and placed a loving hand on Darren's head, then withdrew it quickly at the unexpected sticky sensation. "What did you do?" she asked with a tone of exasperation. Her questioning eyes moved from him to our group and back. I wasn't sure what to say because I didn't want to be the one to rat him out to his mom. As I turned to Owen for an idea, the answer presented itself—all the boys were either gone or escaping as fast as possible. It seemed like a good solution because no harm was done, so I bailed like a nine-year-old and left poor Darren to face his mother's wrath.

Chapter 10

Too Much, Too Soon

T HAT FALL, OWEN'S little brother decided to give soccer a try. Wade was five, a year younger than Owen when he started. Unlike Owen, Wade was very laid back and easygoing. He was also incredibly flexible and could contort his body in ridiculous ways. He was so flexible that it was an issue during one of his early medical checkups. Wade's pediatrician had a name for the condition but advised that no serious health concerns were associated. However, he said that because of low muscle tone, Wade would need to work harder to achieve what other kids his age could do and may be less coordinated. That concerned Judy and me, but we didn't dwell on it because we couldn't change it. Still, we did what we could by encouraging him to be active, which was easy because he was always trying to keep up with his older brother. Playing soccer was part of our "Activity Plan," so we hoped for a positive outcome.

We were lucky. Wade's new coach was great. He had already been through a soccer experience with a previous child and was well prepared. However, he didn't need or want an assistant, so I did not have much contact with him other than a few minutes before games. It was typical to have few practices for Wade's age group; mostly, we showed up on game day, warmed up for a while, and played an intense game. Unfortunately for Wade, the games were not fun. He loved playing soccer with Owen and me but did not like the noise and bedlam accompanying bunch ball. When we watched him play the first game, Judy and I realized that Wade was in over his head.

The game was played early in the morning on a September day. Wade and three teammates probably shivered in their dew-soaked shoes as they squared off against four opposing players. Each team was expected to furnish one coach to co-operatively officiate the game. When both teams were ready, one of the coaches blew a whistle, and the kickoff ensued. As soon as the ball was touched, all four players from each team converged on it. Parents yelled and cheered while eight little tykes pushed and kicked at the ball. There was no passing, no dribbling. The bunch slowly flowed around the field like an amoeba toward one goal and then the other.

At first, Wade charged the ball like everyone else, but the pushing and shoving were too much for him, and after a minute, he popped out of the group. For a few awkward moments, Judy and I watched our son stand outside the center of activity. It looked as if he was isolating himself and avoiding participation. It concerned us, but then something remarkable happened. Wade adjusted and moved to a position on the field where he was in the open but within range of the bunch. He waited, alert, ready, and attentive.

Like magic, the ball squirted from the bunch onto the open field in Wade's direction. He moved toward it, took control, and dribbled at the opponent's goal, covering at least half the field. But as he neared the goal, the bunch caught up to him. Enveloped and surrounded, Wade lost the ball and swam out of the kicking mob.

Again, he took a position on the open field and waited, circling like a satellite, shifting to wherever made the most sense to him while the throng swarmed. Every few minutes, some kid succeeded in blasting the ball out of the bunch, and Wade was there to get it and dribble as far as possible before getting caught.

Although his behavior was initially alarming, he demonstrated the first glimmer of authentic soccer that day. Later, it occurred to me that Wade behaved that way because he'd heard me instruct Owen's team—smart boy. That was a proud thought for me, but we never talked about it, so I didn't know for sure.

The following spring, we opted not to enroll Wade in soccer. He seemed too little and not into the games. Wade was such a compliant child that he would have willingly played on, but more might not have been better. It could have felt like something he had to do instead of something he wanted. Judy and I avoided that tension with our five-year-old because soccer was supposed to be fun. We secretly hoped he would return to the sport because we thought it would benefit him. That was the right decision. He played soccer again, got stronger every season, and learned to love to challenge himself athletically.

Chapter 11

I Get My Wings

SPRING BROUGHT CHANGES to the coaching staff of Owen's team. Coach Dan was too busy with work to attend practices or most games—the head coaching job fell to me. I missed Dan's help, but I felt confident because I had learned the essence of his method.

The other significant change for spring was that Judy and I decided to relocate to the Midwest so we could be closer to extended family. The decision came in March, about the same time we started thinking about soccer again. Consequently, although relocating had nothing to do with soccer, it was always on our minds. The decision had been in the works for a while. Judy and I grew up in neighboring villages and went to the same high school before attending different colleges. When she enrolled in graduate school, I followed her.

We had marvelous adventures when we were childless, but as our lives together progressed, things got more complicated. We wanted our kids to know their grandparents, aunts, uncles, and cousins. We were also concerned about our children attending a big-city high school of one thousand students or more. Ultimately, the allure of relying on grandparents for help sealed the deal.

Judy and I job searched for several years, trying to find a sensible solution where we could both match employers. When my brother contacted me asking if I was interested in returning to the family business, it seemed like an opportunity. I had worked in the business during high school and college, so I knew the basics and what to expect. The move met two of our criteria: a job for me and moving closer to extended families. It also seemed likely that Judy could find a job as a psychologist within the region. The only problem was that the family business had little in common with my career as a research scientist. It was a difficult decision. In the end, I exchanged my research, synthesis, and teaching profession for one of manufacturing, personnel management, and money. It was one of those life-changing decisions I made, never knowing if it was the right thing to do.

OUR LAST SEASON of big-city soccer was great fun. We were a competitive team, and things went well. Our success was less about what I did and mainly about the players. We had several boys on the team who were skilled and excellent leaders. Those boys, Owen included, were well-behaved, worked hard, and led by example. With leaders like that, my job was easy because they set the tempo for practices and games, and others followed. Players came to practice, there were no disagreements, I allotted equal playing time, and we won most of our games. It was a trouble-free group of boys that blended, bonded, and played soccer.

At our last practice, I wanted to do something to reward them, so I began a tradition called Gator Day, where I brought

Gatorade drinks for every player. The beverage selection at the store had been limited when I shopped; only large, twenty-four-ounce bottles were available. With no choice, I got enough for everyone, plus a few extra to avoid disputes over flavors. Halfway through practice, I announced it was time to enjoy the icy-cold beverages, and we headed to the cooler. There was the usual turmoil associated with a bunch of boys competing to get what they wanted, but then things settled down, and we spent a few minutes relaxing on our last day of practice. After about ten minutes, it was time to get back to work. Everyone headed back onto the field except Drew, who gestured toward the extra drinks and asked, "What's going to happen to those?"

"They're extra," I shrugged.

"Can I have another?" Drew asked with a wide-eyed, hopeful look.

I thought for a second and decided that it was the last day of practice—there was no harm in allowing him another drink. As soon as I said, "Sure, you can have another," I realized I had committed an error in judgment. I should have considered the "Drew factor" before making my decision because the grotesque, ill-mannered animal that lurked inside him was barely contained by his skin. When I affirmed that he could have another drink, the animal came out.

Drew's parents taught him that he should not take more until he had consumed what he already had. That posed a problem because he still had half of the original beverage. His solution was to guzzle the remainder in seconds while moving to the cooler. His behavior shocked me because of his reaction speed and the ravenous look in his eyes. Like a wolf gulping down mouthfuls of meat to get its share before other hungry animals arrive at a kill, Drew finished his open Gatorade and then lunged for a second. There was no need for urgency; no one else wanted another because they couldn't finish what they had, but the animal in Drew wanted more. He mercilessly ripped off the top of a green drink and gulped it down. I watched in amazement as he nearly finished it, re-placed the cap, and threw the bottle to the ground. Then he smiled at me, patted his bulging abdomen, and burped before running off to join the other boys. The drink stayed down for about three minutes. Then Drew treated us to yet another out-standing display—The Green Geyser.

THAT SPRING, I successfully coached Owen's soccer team to a winning season. I hadn't given the idea much thought until I was caught off guard after the last game. Our team had a tradition of celebrating the end of each season with a cere-mony to recognize player participation. The order of events varied. Sometimes, we awarded small trophies to every play-er. On other occasions, we had cake and a juice box, but the process always involved calling each player out onto the field one last time to shake the coach's hand and be congratulated. I did that, then moved to join my family to celebrate with a piece of cake.

Before I got to them, one of the parents stopped me. Word of our relocation plan was out, and I was the partici-pant about to be congratulated. They thanked me for my hard work and surprised me with a little clear acrylic trophy about four inches tall, engraved with the team's name and the year. It was small but signified so much. I didn't know what to do for a moment. Then, as I realized that I had succeeded and done the job well, I couldn't hold back. I used two hands to hoist that trophy over my head and pumped it up and down as if it were made from fifty pounds of solid gold. Everyone cheered. Dan was there that day, and I thanked him for teaching me to be a soccer coach. He was gracious and denied that he had done anything, but I knew his influence was strong.

It was a great way to end the season, but our soccer experience continued for years. That July, we put big-city soccer behind us and moved to a land of competitiveness and rigorous rule enforcement. It was the same game, but the approach to soccer in our new home differed, and I had much more to learn.

Andy's Advice ...
for Coaches and Parents Who Have Earned Their Wings

At this stage of development, there is a strong emphasis on skill building. When games become more competitive, it's important to remember that the goal is to have fun, so try to avoid being judgmental. Treating players equally builds trust and team spirit. Some players will accomplish things you never imagined.

For coaches:

1. **Emphasize drills in which every player has a ball.** Maintain a fast pace during practices to encourage constant running.
2. **Employ multiple coaches** to divide the team into small groups so players spend less time standing in lines.
3. **Pit players against each other rather than against coaches** during drills. There may be some unequal matches, but use them as teaching moments so no one is left behind.
4. **Encourage players to communicate effectively** with you because it is difficult for a coach to distinguish if an emotional player is hurt or simply upset.
5. **Stretch and stay fit** to avoid injury.

For parents:

1. **Learn the coach's terminology** to effectively communicate with your player and align your actions with theirs.
2. **Let the referee call the game.** Enforcement of aspects of the game like offside, advantage, and handballs can be confusing until you gain more experience.
3. **Work with your player off the field** because it takes repetition to build strength and skill.
4. **Trust that players will improve.** Value every player because the team will need them in the future.
5. **Encourage your child to be an all-weather player.** Carry a duffle bag with layers for wind, rain, cold, and sun. Consistent play is one key to being great.

Chapter 12

Year 4—Coach Tom

ONCE JUDY AND I knew we were moving, we did what we could to make the transition easy. One of those things was enrolling Owen on a soccer team. We failed to find a club in what would be our hometown but succeeded in identifying one a few miles away. Judy followed up with a phone call and confirmed that Owen would be able to get on a team. That done, nothing was left for us to do except move our family and all our possessions 1,000 miles, get settled, and show up for practice on the first day. Easy peasy—except it wasn't.

We arrived at our new home during the last week in July. The move went as planned; nothing was broken or damaged. The street in front of our house was newly paved and seemed welcoming. The house was a fixer-upper but was new to us, and our kids looked past the flaws. So, with fresh pavement on which to ride bikes and a fenced-in backyard to keep little Megan from wandering off, we settled in.

The demographics of our new neighborhood were mature; no other kids lived on our block. But it was summer, and there were things to do, like emptying moving boxes, going to the beach, and getting reacquainted with extended family.

The time went fast. In a few short weeks, it was soccer season again.

OWEN AND I arrived at the first practice on a hot, sunny Saturday morning in August. The soccer complex was on the edge of town and surrounded by cornfields and woodlots. It was a nice facility with a playground, pavilion, bathrooms, and drinking water. The only thing that it didn't have was activity. I felt uneasy as car after car pulled into the parking lot and stopped only long enough to let a player out, then drove away. The parking lot was located uphill from the soccer fields. From our vantage point, it was clear that no one was around except our coach and a few players. I was surprised that all the other parents dropped and ditched their offspring. I wasn't comfortable doing that, although I didn't say anything to Owen. We both grabbed our water bottles and followed the others to the field.

I got a weird vibe from Coach Tom the moment I met him. I can't explain it. It was a solid first impression that I tried not to embrace because I didn't know the man. I don't know what it was about him that raised my concern. It could have been his welcome speech in which he announced that he was not Hitler but was a strong disciplinarian. That got my attention, but on the first day of practice, I gave him the benefit of the doubt. We chatted a bit, and I told him I had previous coaching experience and was willing to help. He said he didn't need me because his older son would assist. I thought it odd that his older son was not at practice that day. I also thought it was foolish of him to turn away help because another coach allowed him to break practice down into small groups so that players got more touches on the ball. That was how Dan and I ran things; it worked well, but Tom didn't want my help, and I didn't argue. Instead, I stepped back and explored the park while keeping one eye on the activities until the practice was over.

Coach Tom's first practice was uninspiring and dull. It started with each player jogging twice around the perimeter of the soccer field while practicing the skip dribble, a skill unfamiliar to all the players, including Owen. Since nobody knew how to do the skip dribble, it degraded into an awkward jog twice around the field without any encouragement or coaching. After that, Coach Tom moved on to a 1v10 drill with the entire team in a circle around him. One by one, Tom picked a player and passed them the ball, then they passed back. Ten players and one ball made for a painfully slow drill—I felt sorry for the team because they looked hot and bored. The next activity gave me a flashback to the butt-shielding tie-dyed dad. Coach Tom instructed each player to stand in a single line until it was their turn to dribble a ball past him; Tom won every challenge, took the ball, then tortured and embarrassed them while the rest of the team looked on. Practice finished with a scrimmage, and I met Owen at the parking lot. He seemed frustrated and defeated.

I felt bad. Judy and I had hoped that soccer in the bucolic Midwest would be fun and consistent with our previous experience. But it was very different. There was no drink or snack schedule, I wasn't involved in coaching, and Coach Tom was intimidating instead of charismatic. It seemed like it was going to be a long season.

We practiced twice weekly. As the pregame weeks went

by, Owen got acquainted with his teammates, and things fell into a soccer routine, but Coach Tom's aptitude for coaching did not improve. The team was coed, which didn't matter to Owen or me, but the overall skill level was lower than what we were accustomed to. Owen was the most capable player at every position. The one player who gave him a run for his money was the coach's son, Charlie, who wanted to play forward and score goals. Fortunately, Owen preferred defending and bringing the ball up the field. Owen's ability with the soccer ball made him popular with most other players on the team, but Charlie never warmed up to him. The problem was that Owen's skill with the ball made him most qualified to play forward in Coach Tom's eyes, which demoted Charlie to other positions. As the first game loomed, I hoped that everything would work out.

MUCH WAS UNSPOKEN between Owen and me on the day of our first game; everything seemed different. Both of us were uneasy as we headed separate ways at the soccer field. In our previous experience, players and parents from each team sat on the same side of the pitch. That convention complicated coaching because boisterous fans could be a distraction, but it afforded opportunities for parents to learn the game and interact with the team. Consequently, coaches and parents knew each other well. In our new league, players and parents occupied opposite sides of the field. Players were on their own with the coach, and parents, most of whom knew nothing about soccer, were far away. Parents rarely interacted with coaches; when they did, it was always formal. I was not a coach, so my place was with the parents. I recognized a couple of them from my high school days. As we became reacquainted, they admitted that they knew nothing about soccer. So, I became their soccer translator.

As the teams prepared for the start of the game, the gravity of the situation became apparent to me. From my vantage across the field, I watched Coach Tom give the team his pregame speech, then move to a bench on the sideline and sit down. I don't blush very often—about once every decade—but on that day, I felt my face flush. I unconsciously looked down at the ground with shame and disappointment because I thought I had failed Owen and things would get worse. Tom mentioned to me on one occasion that coaches couldn't do much during a game because it was all up to the players.

When I heard him say it, I wondered if he was serious. I agreed with his point regarding individual player ability. Still, I knew from experience that teams needed to be coached in real time during games because things happened differently compared to practices. Judy often remarked that despite my inexperience, I was more adept than Coach Dan at making adjustments during a game. However, as I watched our team prepare to play their first game, none of my abilities mattered because I was on the wrong sideline—the parents' sideline. Our team took the field and then took a beating. Owen worked and tried to make things happen, but his teammates lacked the skill and ability to play together. Through it all, Coach Tom sat silently on the bench.

When it was over, I walked across the field to meet Owen. He grabbed his water bottle, and we headed down the sideline to the parking lot together. There was nothing to say. He was angry, I was angry—but what could I do? I was not the coach, and one defeat was not enough to convince anyone that Coach Tom did not know what he was doing. "We have to keep trying and hope that the team gets better," was the only thing I could think to say on the way home.

NOTHING IMPROVED THE following week. The game's outcome was the same as the first, and I became more frustrated by Tom's coaching style of divorcing himself from the team. I wondered if he would do the same thing if they were winning. On the morning of the third game, there was a noticeable change in Owen's attitude about soccer. By that point, he had been subjected to Coach Tom's demeaning style for five weeks, which took its toll. His excitement and enthusiasm for playing soccer were gone. As we stood in our kitchen preparing to leave for the game, Owen said the words that I thought he would never say. I never even considered it; never thought it would be a problem in a million years.

"I don't want to play soccer."

Judy and I both heard it. He didn't say anything else, probably because it was all he could manage without tears, but the silence in the room spoke volumes. It was heartbreaking because I knew how much he loved playing the game. I hadn't realized how bad the situation was until then, but I did not want him to quit. After a pause, I replied, "Let's see how the game goes. Then we will figure something out." That was all it took; Owen complied.

The game was the same as the others. There were a few bright moments when Owen had success moving the ball against the other team, and his team had some success scoring, but it wasn't the team effort or the losing that was the problem; it was Coach Tom's style and attitude that had worn Owen down.

After the game, one of the boys invited Owen over for the afternoon. As I walked back to the parking lot across the expanse of the nearly deserted soccer complex, a man approached me. It was the president of the Soccer Club. I had met him previously, and he remembered me because I told him about my coaching experience. He was friendly and asked, "How's it going?" as he tipped his head toward the soccer field.

I tried to make my words calm and measured. "Not so good," I said, adding, "I think Tom needs some help."

The president smiled and laughed nervously, then replied, "Well, you could volunteer to help him."

I couldn't believe what I heard because I had offered to help. I tried not to show anger and thought, *Maybe this is my chance.*

I straightened my posture, checked my emotion, looked the president straight in the eyes, and spoke in a solemn and determined voice, "I did offer to help. Tom turned me down."

The president was embarrassed by my retort and promised to talk to Tom. I thanked him and continued to the car; he continued to the soccer field, where Tom was still finishing up. That evening, I received a phone call from the president informing me that Tom had forgotten my offer of assistance and that he welcomed my help. I agreed to start at the next practice and hung up the phone in disbelief but with a glimmer of hope. It was much easier to get Owen to go to the next practice.

Chapter 13

New Hope

OWEN AND I arrived early at my new coaching assignment, but it didn't make things any less awkward. As I approached Coach Tom on that first day of our new relationship, he strode toward me with an air of confrontation and almost shouted, "Well, what are we doing today?" The vibe I got on the first day of practice was still there, but a layer of irritation intensified Tom's demeanor. His abrupt welcome surprised me because I intended to contribute, not take over.

I deliberated for a moment. "I think we should work on defense. I have a good drill in mind," I said.

Coach Tom backed off a little. "Okay. Then maybe we can finish with one of mine."

"That'd be great," I responded, relieved to have reduced the tension.

While Tom sent the team out to complete their usual two-lap warmup, I set up cones and explained the agenda.

Defense was one of the easiest things to teach a naive soccer team because it is simple: defenders must block the attacker's path to the goal. I put up two sets of cones, one for Tom and one for me, and positioned players on each. Then I directed the first player in line to be a defender and instructed them to stand between two more cones arranged as a gate-way—the path to the goal. The remaining players in line were attackers whose task was to dribble a ball through the gate. The defender's job was to stop them. I explained basic defensive technique, then let the magic happen.

My approach was to let everybody have a try, then reinforce that a defender's responsibility was to stop the attacker's advance, to get in their way, and keep pressuring until the opponent made a mistake. The drill constrained defender movement: they couldn't escape my oversight or their opponent, so they had to attempt the task. Most players succeeded. A stubborn few could not break natural tendencies, but even those improved with time. The amazing thing was how quickly players learned. On the first try, attackers usually won and succeeded in dribbling through the cones, but that changed quickly. Soon, defenders were winning. It was messy and ugly, but some players, especially instinctive defenders, improved. After about twenty minutes, I handed things over to Coach Tom.

My contribution to the next practice was the same—I conducted a defensive drill and exposed players to an increasingly realistic progression. They improved, and there was a ray of hope for the next game.

THAT WEEKEND I joined Owen and the rest of the team on the players' sideline. I asked Tom if I could call in some commands to players during the game. He consented, so I coached during times of transition when we needed to get back on defense quickly. I was reserved and did less than I

wanted for fear of exceeding my allowance. The team struggled to score, but our defense improved. Once again, Tom
sat silently on the bench during the game—until halftime.
He chose to speak then, which was unfortunate because he
gave the most demeaning, spirit-crushing, self-esteem-de-
stroying speech I ever experienced. I only recall the first three
sentences.

"You kids are playing like losers," said Coach Tom.
"Losers, losers, losers. If you want to be losers, keep playing
like losers."

Everything after that was a blur because I couldn't believe what I heard. I felt flush with anger and embarrassment.
I had a vague awareness that I clenched my fists. My enraged
mind raced as I tried to stay composed and figure out what
to do as Tom excoriated our team of nine-year-old boys and
girls. No one deserved to be lectured that way at a Saturday
afternoon recreational soccer game. Fortunately, he emphasized his disgust for his team's performance by abruptly ending his diatribe. Then he instructed them to get a drink and
prepare for the second half. Coach Tom's words failed to motivate; the second half was similar to the first. When it was
over, Owen and I rendezvoused with Judy, Wade, and Megan
and got out of there.

THE FOLLOWING WEEK was our second-to-last game,
and I was prepared. Somehow, I persuaded Tom to change
Owen's position from forward to defender, which allowed us
to shore up our defense and move the ball away from the
goal. Tom moved his son to Owen's vacant position. That

arrangement made us much more competitive. During the game, I made more calls from the sideline, which kept our players on track. At one point, Tom commented about how much I was coaching. He was irritated and passive-aggressive, so I toned my activity down but didn't stop because I could see that I was helping the team. We scored a couple of goals in the first half, and Tom managed a somewhat positive halftime speech. We didn't win, but we made a respectable effort.

Chapter 14

A Plan for the Future

BECAUSE OF THE Coach Tom catastrophe, Judy and I developed a plan to extract Owen from the situation after the conclusion of the fall season and get him onto a team in our local community. Our local Soccer Club did not have a website, so we couldn't identify it before we moved to the area. But since then, Judy had become acquainted with a mom whose son played on the team. Because of her research, we had an alternative.

Owen had also become friends with several players on the team and was excited to join them. The problem was that the team was packed, and the coaches didn't want more participants. I knew that a lot could change between fall and spring and that a spot would probably be available for Owen. I also knew that no coach in his right mind would turn Owen away because of his above-average ability to move the ball.

With fingers crossed, I called the coach and arranged a "tryout" for Owen. It was informal. We showed up for practice, and Owen participated. The coaches (there were two) liked what they saw and said there would be a spot for Owen in the spring. They seemed like nice guys. There was no weird vibe or Hitler speech. I liked them, and Owen liked the team.

It seemed like there was a chance we could rekindle our old soccer magic in our new home.

Chapter 15

Self-Respect Returns

THE LAST WEEK of practice with Coach Tom was a repeat. I added new material, and the team continued to improve. As we wrapped up the last practice, Owen asked me if he could play goalkeeper in the game. He confided that he had made the request to Coach Tom several times, but his pleas were unsuccessful.

Owen's request was not out of line. Coach Dan and I always mixed player positions, so everyone had exposure to each role. However, Coach Tom had a different philosophy. I was concerned about raising Tom's ire, but with only one game to go, I took a chance and inquired on Owen's behalf. Tom found it more difficult to ignore an adult's request than a child's—he agreed. With that change, the conditions of our last game were set. Owen would be in the goal for the first half and then play defender during the second. The circumstances were what Owen and I wanted—and it was going to be spectacular!

THE SEASON'S LAST game was always a great relief for me—relief that I had made it through the season, that no one was seriously injured, and that the obligations would be over soon, no matter the outcome. Our family went to the game with a brighter outlook. Owen and I went to the players' side of the field; Judy, Wade, and Megan departed for the parents' side but were commandeered by Megan to the playground. Consequently, the events on that chilly October day were shared only by Owen and me.

As we warmed up, a gray sky hinted at rain and gave the field an unusually dark green hue that contrasted with white field markings. For protection against the elements, Owen wore a knit cap and a sweatshirt under his jersey, making him look bulky and thick when he moved. During the first half, the teams were evenly matched. Our defenders did an excellent job challenging the other team and kicking the ball away. Some weak shots got through the defense, but Owen, who was the goalkeeper, swept them up easily. Toward the end of the first half, we pressed near the other team's goal when they intercepted and broke away. One player with the ball charged across the centerline. He bolted past our defenders and was alone—only Owen stood in his way.

"Oh no," I thought as I watched the developing duel. It was significant because Owen and I had been through a lot that autumn. With each step, the breakaway kid threatened the success that we had worked to achieve. Our team had improved, and so had Owen's attitude since I began coaching. I wanted to win badly, not just for Owen but for every kid on the team. We all needed a win to replace an abysmal experience with something tolerable. We needed a good memory. Those thoughts were in my mind as the player from the other team crossed midfield and ran at the goal with only Owen to stop him.

But Owen was ready.

He used a tactic Coach Dan and I taught and charged out from the goal as the attacker approached the portion of the field where a goalkeeper could use their hands. The tactic worked because it was better for a young keeper to attack an opponent than to let them shoot. Owen's timing was perfect. He blocked the attacker's path, looming closer with each step. Before the kid could react, Owen was at his feet with his hands on the ball.

It was a spectacular save. Both sidelines erupted with cheers and applause. I spontaneously yelled, "Monster," because that was what Owen looked like in his cold-weather gear—a bulky, fearless soccer monster. The save was huge!

Owen stayed focused on the game. He held the ball for a few seconds, then dropkicked it to an open teammate. A few minutes later, the chain of events repeated. The outcome was the same—another great save. We went into halftime tied 0-0, and Coach Tom did not destroy morale with a demoralizing speech. I was optimistic about the second half because we had weathered the best the other team could throw at us. With Owen moving to the field as a defender for the rest of the game, we were in an unusually good position.

The teams were evenly matched during the first half when Owen was in the goal. That parity changed when Owen began to exert his influence on the field. His position was sweeper, the last line of defense before our goalkeeper. He could score from that position, though it was unlikely. Dan and I had always encouraged players to flex out of their roles and "make a run" if they got the chance. The idea was that regardless of position, a player should carry the ball until challenged, then pass to a teammate, and return to where they belonged, but if they could move the ball to the goal, that was even better.

The other team had the kickoff to begin the second half. They did that successfully and pushed their attack to our goal. That was Owen's territory, and he defended it well. About two minutes into the second half, he intercepted the ball and counterattacked on the run. The opposing team had crept up and out of position; after a few steps, Owen was alone with the ball. As he ran the length of the field, only the opposing goalkeeper remained, and they were not well-trained. The keeper waited as Owen dribbled closer—the goal was easy. Owen kicked an accurate ground ball into the corner of the net and jogged back to our side of the field while parents and players cheered. We were ahead 1-0 and leading a game for the first time all season.

There was some high-fiving. Then, as the other team prepared to kick off, I urged players to get their focus back and be ready to play. It worked, and they settled down—or at least Owen did. A few minutes later, he had another break-away at midfield. He stole the ball from a player and was almost immediately beyond everyone except the goalkeeper. As before, he closed the distance and kicked in an easy goal. That was the game changer for me. At that point, I knew we would win, barring some bizarre chain of events unleashed upon us. Fortunately, the heavens did not open, and locusts did not descend. Neither team was able to score another goal before time expired.

THERE WAS NOTHING as sweet as winning the last game of the season, especially if it was the only win. It felt great, though I felt a pang of sympathy for the other team. I wondered if they had gone winless. Were their hopes of winning the last game smashed as they watched my son get two tremendous saves in the first half and score twice in the second? I hoped not, but my sympathetic musings hinted at an imbalance that often existed between competitiveness and fun in rec soccer. Intense competition was a path to excellence, but too much of it diminished sportsmanship, fairness, and inclusiveness. Conversely, too much fun engendered a lack of discipline, poor work ethic, and low performance standards. Finding a balance between those emphases wasn't easy; Coach Tom didn't have the right blend for Owen, Judy, and me.

The following February, a few weeks before spring soccer started, I called Coach Tom and told him that Owen would not return. I owed him a call because players signed up annually to play on the same team for fall and spring. He objected initially, telling me that the league had rules to prevent players from changing teams. He was right. The rules were there to prevent players from abandoning teams doing poorly and gravitating toward those doing well. It was a good policy that I agreed with, but I could not get the "loser, loser, loser" speech out of my head. I was sure that the league had a policy against that too. I didn't feel obligated to stay because we were not leaving to escape a losing team; we were going because we disagreed with Tom's coaching style. I didn't argue with him, and I didn't feel compelled to criticize. He wasn't happy with our departure but couldn't change our decision. I was glad it was over. Whatever was ahead of us had to be better than what we left behind.

Andy's Advice ... on Avoiding Conflict

It is easy to criticize a coach. Remember that the coach is a volunteer, may be inexperienced, and might not have sought their role. Your child's behavior is a good indicator of coach performance, but consider other factors because coaches push players out of their comfort zones. If you suspect a coach's philosophy conflicts with yours, try to get more involved so you can evaluate and have input.

For coaches:

1. **Avoid favoritism.** Administer reprimands and rewards consistently. Inconsistent coaches lose the respect of those they treat unfairly.
2. **Let *learning by doing* be your mantra.** Overcome weaknesses on your team with new skills and drills instead of words.
3. **Be positive.** Build on what players are doing well and baby-step your way to a better team. Negative comments cause a loss of self-esteem, leading to decreased attendance and performance.
4. **Stay involved during the game** by coaching from the sideline using keywords introduced at practices.
5. **Clearly state expectations for attendance and participation.** Be flexible, but withhold playing time to achieve compliance. If an angry parent confronts you, remain calm and explain your reasoning.

For parents:

1. **Do your homework** before enrolling your child on a team. Inquire about the coach's demeanor, player attitudes, fundraising requirements, and tournament participation.
2. **Have faith that conditions will improve** when bad things happen. As long as your player is having fun, encourage them to continue. The departure of capable players can feel like a devastating loss, but it allows others to step up.

3. **Build a relationship with the coach.** Participating as an assistant is the best way to observe the coach's behavior and allows you to learn from someone with more experience.

4. **The win/loss record is just one benchmark of success.** When evaluating a coach, consider other measures like player attitude, skill development, confidence, and teamwork.

5. **Consider withdrawing from the team** if the relationship with the coach is irreparable and your child demonstrates avoidance or a loss of self-esteem. Discuss the decision with your player so they understand why leaving the team is acceptable.

Chapter 16

Return to Normality

OUR SPRING SOCCER experience with a new team was what we hoped for—the coaches were easygoing, and the players welcomed Owen. He found a role as a defender and developed an ability to work with the head coach's son, who played forward. Together, they moved the ball away from our goal, transitioned to attack, and finished by scoring on many occasions. That sort of play made Owen a welcome asset and dissolved his new-kid status among his teammates.

Our easy-peasy plan to move the family 1,000 miles and get Owen involved in soccer took longer and was more difficult than we anticipated, but it ultimately worked out. My role in Owen's soccer activities was shrinking. His team already had two coaches; they didn't need a third. However, I wanted to do something to stay involved, so I volunteered to help at practices. I retrieved poorly kicked soccer balls and managed fidgety boys so the coaches could maximize instruction. I had it easy during games and watched from the parents' side of the field. It was a nice break—the only one for years to come because Wade was just getting started.

Chapter 17

Year 5–Culture Shock

COACHING SOCCER IN my home state was more complicated than I expected. There were the usual challenges related to players, as well as additional problems associated with parents, coaches, and the Soccer Club. The last three entities were nearly invisible in the big city but often needed attention in our new, closely-knit rural soccer league.

I volunteered to coach Wade's team when we registered him and Owen for the upcoming fall season. Two weeks before the start of that season, I received a phone call inviting me to attend a coaches' meeting. So, on a quiet evening in early August, I went to the grade school and followed the trickle of coaches entering the building. The meeting was called to order by Dawn, the president of the club. She was flanked on one side by five men and women who comprised the rest of the club's Soccer Board. I was one of about fifteen coaches in the audience, most of whom were men.

As the meeting proceeded, it became clear that there was tension in the room. Certain men in the audience were trying to backseat drive the discussion. They interrupted Dawn to ask questions to be addressed further down the agenda or were argumentative and sarcastic. At one point, a man joked with another, then crossed the room to share a high five.

That was my introduction to soccer zealots, whom I had never encountered before. In the big city, teams were competitive, but everyone was from the same metropolitan area. The registration process moved players around, so some opposing players became familiar, but their teams were ever-changing. That ambiguity diffused the competitiveness of games, which were never about beating the Crocodiles from the south side or the Rangers from the east side.

In the rural Midwest, every team hailed from a different town, and civic pride intensified the competitive spirit of each event. This fervor seeped into the actions of parents, coaches, referees, and soccer clubs, each distinctly influenced by their dedication to their local communities. High-school rivalries elevated the significance of matches played by seven-year-olds. Some coaches played to win above all else, which meant that weak players sat on the bench during games unless a clear victory was at hand. Those ultra-competitive coaches and some parents formed the core of the soccer zealots. They ensured that the rules were enforced to their advantage, sometimes going so far as to overstep their authority and implement a rule where none existed, but always reserving a special dispensation for themselves or specific friends. The soccer zealots sought power to achieve what they wanted; many were club presidents. From that vantage point, they could bend the rules and stack rosters to concentrate high-ability players on teams, wave through coaches who lacked background checks, or relax requirements that two adults be present at practices. There were good reasons for those rules. They were intended to prevent teams from obtaining an unfair advantage and to keep the environment safe. But those limits were easily circumvented. The result was a sugarcoated authoritarian regime that was supportive if demands were met; otherwise, it was vindictive.

I did not understand the influence of zealots on small-town soccer. I just sat on my folding chair and observed the tense push-pull of rule presentation and eye-rolling. Nearly everyone in the meeting was new to me, so it was an evening of first impressions. I thought Dawn did a good job. She was well-organized and tried to get through the material quickly. I suspected that the distracting behavior by men in the audience was due to chauvinism and that they would have been more respectful if the club president had been male. If not for the interruptions, it would have been a short meeting, but the people in the audience who had the least to say did most of the talking. The meeting adjourned after a little more than an hour. I went home with a list of players on Wade's team, a game schedule, a bag of soccer equipment, and my enrollment in a soccer clinic the following week.

THE SOCCER CLINIC was different from my previous experience, which was introductory and taught in a classroom by a soccer club member. The new clinic was held in a gymnasium and led by a coach with an interesting British accent and credentials from a local university. He was charismatic and thoroughly introduced the philosophy of coaching, responsibilities, and basic game concepts for novice coaches. During the last half of the clinic, he took on the role of coach, and the attendees became players. We were "learning by doing" as he led us through basic soccer drills. I was frustrated because much of what he covered was very basic. Still, some of the material was useful, and I jotted down notes of things I could implement for Wade's team.

At the end of the simulated practice, he had one last piece of advice. "Coaches don't have much influence on the outcome of the game. It is up to the players."

I had heard that before from Coach Tom. On the surface, it made sense. For me, the advice was encouraging but unrealistic. It relieved some pressure associated with my new responsibility to Wade and his teammates. I suspected that was the intent, but my happy feeling only lasted until the first practice. In reality, coaching was time-consuming and difficult. I was alone without a mentor or knowledgeable colleague, translating what I knew about soccer into something seven-year-olds could accomplish. I had already been through the process with Owen; that experience was my starting point.

Chapter 18

Soccer on the Serengeti

WADE'S FIRST PRACTICE served two purposes: getting players together and introducing myself to parents. I was halfway from the parking lot to the soccer field when the skinniest kid I had ever seen appeared at my side. He was small for his age and so lean that bones stuck out all over—cheekbones, elbows, kneecaps. With a smattering of freckles on his face, large teeth, and a short clipper cut, he looked like a speckled, walking skeleton. The skeleton spoke with a high but confident voice,

"Hi, coach. My name's William, and I can run like a cheetah."

He thrust his hand out and waited for me to accept his offer. I was surprised and slightly shocked by the appearance of the bony sprite in front of me and the confident introduction. It was unusual behavior for a seven-year-old. I dropped my gear and shook his hand, "I'm Andy. Glad to meet you." We regarded each other for a moment, and then, without another word, William dashed off. As I turned to pick up the gear, his dad appeared, smiling and laughing, with his hand extended. We made introductions, and I briefly talked with a larger version of William, though not nearly so lean.

"He loves to play," his dad confirmed, then he turned to go back to his truck, and I continued to practice.

I took up a position near the edge of our playing field to greet other players and parents. One by one, I introduced myself, sent players onto the field, and chatted with parents as I waited for people to arrive. When the pace of arrivals slowed, my thoughts turned to wrapping up the meeting. I turned toward the parking lot to check for latecomers. One woman walked toward me, with her son following a few paces behind. She got my attention because she walked purposefully and exuded an aura of pure, unbending determination. I steadied myself as if I was being charged by an angry lioness protecting her cub on the Serengeti plain—don't run, don't show fear, don't make direct eye contact, and adopt a calming demeanor.

She bypassed my handshake and roared, "My son doesn't respond well to negative criticism." Her son dashed off to join the other players on the field; I faced the beast alone.

"Hi, I'm Andy," I responded, then paused and asked myself, *What would Coach Dan do?* Dan was always smiling and mellow, so I smiled and replied, "There is almost always something good about what a player does. I encourage what they are doing well and build on it." It was the right thing to say because the lioness hesitated, then veered off, apparently satisfied that her cub was not in danger. I was relieved and surprised at how well I handled the potential confrontation. I said the right thing to diffuse the situation and wondered how the idea popped into my head.

Later, I realized that what I said wasn't just a defense mechanism but my philosophy of coaching players. I saw how negative coaching destroyed Owen's love of soccer.

The experience taught me that being positive was a better approach. It provided something to build on—success, even if we lost a game. Encouraging players helped them baby-step their way to improving skills and self-confidence. That confidence translated into trust—trust in themselves and trust in me.

The lioness's son's name was Alan. Alan needed self-confidence. In time, Alan would learn to trust me, and I would push him to improve his play and accomplish things that he thought impossible. The cub would grow.

Chapter 19

A New Routine

WITH THE BEGINNING of the season behind us, the Beers family fell into a fall soccer routine. Owen practiced on Wednesdays and Fridays, and Wade on Tuesdays and Thursdays. I went to all of them.

Owen's coaches, Henry and Felix, had a coaching style that was free and easy. Their practices were scrimmages. That worked because their all-boys team was playing in a coed league. On average, they were faster and more aggressive than most coed teams and didn't need much coaching to win. I watched and learned what I could.

Owen's coaches emphasized position assignments and responsibilities in preparation for games. Their advice was valuable to me because they offered a different perspective. They also worked on corner kicks and penalty kicks. What they didn't do was spend time building skills. There were no 1v1 or ball-handling drills. That didn't bode well for their team's future because weak players did not improve. Instead, they were assigned secondary roles and used to fill gaps on the field, but they seemed to vanish in games because more aggressive, skilled players outworked them. In years ahead, as Owen's team transitioned from 6v6 to 8v8 and then to

11v11 players, those struggling teammates became the team's downfall.

THE SECOND PRACTICE with Wade's team was an opportunity to evaluate player ability. My first impression was that they seemed like really nice kids—well-behaved, quiet, and obedient. There was none of the fidgety, hyperactive behavior that was common on Owen's team. That was good, but the downside was that there wasn't an aggressive bone in them. They were not quick to the ball and lacked competitiveness. My previous experience with Owen when he was Wade's age was the yardstick for comparison, and the skill deficit worried me. I hoped it was due to a regional difference in soccer ability. The skill level may have been higher in the big city because the soccer program was more active. The parents I consulted didn't have much to offer. They were incredibly grateful I was coaching and relieved that the responsibility didn't fall on their shoulders. Some had previously coached the team in an "in-house" program that emphasized playing and having fun; there were no formal games. That was behind us. I wished the parents had done a little less playing and more skill-building because I was facing the challenge of whipping the team into condition to play 5v5 soccer with a goalkeeper. I started with the basics: right foot, left foot, dribbling, passing, and shooting. I also introduced the concept of positions (forwards and defenders). There wasn't much time; we squeezed in two practices before our first game.

I WAS HOPEFUL but not confident on game day. Everything depended on whether the regional level of skill matched our ability. Wade and I arrived early to get organized on the sideline and be a beacon for parents and players. As we waited, I watched the opposing coach prepare. She was an imposing woman. Short and stout, she moved and spoke with the authority of an army general, and her team responded when she barked out commands. I grew concerned that I was outclassed when she laid down carpet squares for her players—that was unusual. As game time approached, both teams warmed up, then returned to the sideline to finish preparations. There was a flurry of shoestring tying and confusion about ownership of identical-looking disposable water bottles. Then I called the group together to get them focused. I reinforced what we worked on during practice and encouraged them to have fun. When the referee called us to the field, I sent my enthusiastic players onto the pitch, and kickoff ensued.

At that age level, the ball was kicked off the field frequently. Each occasion was an opportunity to substitute players on the field. Some coaches swapped entire teams, others just a few. My rival exchanged two players at a time. She shouted, "Front line!" and two players sitting on carpet squares jumped up and ran onto the field as their counterparts ran off. A few minutes later, "Back line!" was ordered, and the other players jumped up. It was intimidating but effective and different from my method, which was more conversational. I told players their positions and whom to send out, then they went in as directed by the referee. Our opponents were well trained—they rolled over us. I was impressed by their discipline, but they were victorious because a few players were more aggressive and beat us to the ball. Those were things that we could learn.

Most players were aware that we lost the game. Before I spoke to the team about the outcome, I considered my options because what I said could influence how they took the loss. In reality, it was an almost meaningless game played by a bunch of kids under eight years old. There was no point in criticizing them and making the loss more memorable, so I stayed positive: "We played well today, but there are a few things we can do better. We'll work on them at the next practice. I'm proud that you did not give up when we fell behind. It's good to get that first game behind us. Now we know what to expect." I looked at the team and asked, "Any questions?" There were none, so I said, "Everybody in," and extended my arm and closed fist. I waited for each player to put their hand on top of mine, then I shouted, "Bulldogs on three. One, two, three ..." The team might have been timid during games, but they weren't in the huddle. They shouted, "Bulldogs!" and I sent them home. As I collected gear, Judy reclaimed Megan from the playground then met Wade and me near the parking lot. She smiled and congratulated us, "One down, six games to go."

Chapter 20

The Game in the Bleachers

OWEN'S GAMES WERE usually played in the afternoon. I was not his coach, so I sat with Judy on the parents' sideline. Owen played on a larger field than Wade, and the parents' competitiveness increased accordingly. It was awkward to be a coach and sit with parents. Most were there to watch their son play; an annoying few were there to coach the team.

One dad was particularly aggravating. His son, Liam, was on the team but was constantly unfocused during practices. I suspected Liam was there because his parents thought it would be good for him, but all he did was mess around. During games, he spent a significant amount of time on the bench. When Liam's turn came, he struggled because his skills were weak. Consequently, his frustrated dad took it out on the rest of the team. He had played soccer and did not yell things like "Get the ball." Instead, he yelled soccer-related terms. "Go to" encouraged players to run to the ball quickly to gain possession. "Don't chase" reminded players not to pursue faster opponents who had the ball but to anticipate where they were going and cut them off. "Mark up" urged individuals to attend to unguarded adversaries. All those phrases were relatively new to me. I didn't always understand what he meant. Still, I could tell his words were well-timed and constructive, and players needed to embrace his advice. But there were two challenges.

First, Henry and Felix were not reinforcing the same concepts or using the same terms, so players didn't know what Liam's dad was encouraging them to do. From the players' perspective he was a distraction—a big, obnoxious guy with a booming voice on the parents' side of the field who was yelling out calls. The other challenge was that Liam's dad lacked authority. Henry and Felix frequently told players to ignore advice from parents because it was often inconsistent with what they wanted players to accomplish. Armed with that stamp of approval, the ten-year-old boys did what they typically do when confronted by an anonymous, loud, angry-sounding adult. They ignored him. He wasted his effort, and nothing changed except for what I learned by listening to him. Most of the time, Owen's team was victorious. On those occasions, the coaching dads kept their comments relatively low-key. Sometimes, though, things didn't go well. Then the frustrated yelling was irritating.

The utterly indifferent parents were at the other end of the spectrum from the coaching dads. One man stood out. He was a doctor who came to games occasionally and read a paperback novel amidst cheering parents. He left an impression on me because it had to be an uncomfortable and distracting environment in which to read. Still, he attempted it on painfully hard aluminum bleachers. He didn't watch the game or converse with other parents but sat, ostensibly reading intently—a pillar of disinterest. I often wondered why he didn't sit in his car, which would have been more comfortable and less conspicuous. The glass half full was that at least he was there. If his son were injured, he would have been available for consultation. However, like Liam, his son was a distracted player who put forth little effort—a son with a lack of focus, a father with a lack of interest.

The perfect parenting middle ground between wannabe coaches and uninterested parents depends on a variety of conditions. There is a broad range of acceptable solutions—from showing interest but letting players play, to being a boisterous but respectful fan. Games are difficult for players because they feel pressure to perform and win. Parents with high or unrealistic expectations increase that pressure, making it more likely that a player will lose interest or have a negative experience. On the other hand, indifferent parents who allow unmotivated players to participate for the sake of hanging out with friends are not doing their children any favors. It is a parent's responsibility to teach their child that if they enroll in a team sport, they should do their best to contribute because their teammates rely on them. Unmotivated players who don't understand that expectation will be a source of discord because coaches and teammates will resent their lack of effort.

Parents feel a thrill when they see their child succeed and receive recognition for great athleticism or skill. But parents need to remember that rec soccer games are not played for their benefit. The perfect middle ground for parental behavior depends on the child. Some players will embrace the opportunity to play and work to improve without prompting; others will be more hesitant and may require encouragement. Forcing a child to participate because a parent contends that it is good for them is not as productive as encouraging a child to play because they might like the game. Giving a child the opportunity to decide whether or not to participate in a sport lays the foundation for the commitment that will help them succeed.

Parental behavior away from the field is as important as how they conduct themselves on the sideline because success doesn't magically happen on game day. It's the product of hard work, dedication, and teamwork throughout the season. A well-prepared player knows what to do on the field without prompting from the bench or the bleachers. If that goal is achieved, the adults have done their jobs regardless of a game's outcome.

Chapter 21

The Paradox of Coaching Realized

UNLIKE OWEN'S, WADE'S coed team comprised girls and boys. Both genders seemed roughly equal in ability—if there was a difference, the girls got the edge because many of our tall, lanky boys struggled with coordination and quickness. Our biggest challenge was that we were average. We didn't have a dominant player that excelled at some aspect of the game. It was a hard pill for me to swallow. I knew it would be a long soccer season, but I thought that if I could get players to come to practice and work, they would learn the skills to become a winning team. I wasn't wrong— we won our third game that season. It wasn't spectacular or dominating or a colossal comeback. There was no Disney moment. Our average seven-year-olds went toe-to-toe with the opposing average seven-year-olds, and we won.

It felt good to win. It's human nature to want to win. We are born with an instinct to pursue goals. The behavior starts when we are newborns with an urge to seek warmth and suckle, and ends with our last breath. Between those landmarks, we meet challenges daily and live our lives. Some goals are perceived as trivial, others as momentous, depending on how much preparation is required to attain them. When we succeed, a chemical chain reaction in our brain produces feelings of pleasure, joy, and satisfaction. The memory of those emotions pushes us to continue to strive for what we want.

Parents want their children to have fun. Consequently, winning in rec sports is anticipated. The win-loss record of their child's soccer team is how many parents evaluate success. I knew that when our team left the field and went home, the first question that nearly every player had to answer was, "Did you win?" I suspected that a "yes" elicited a reaction of satisfaction and a "no" of disappointment. I doubted that when the latter response was given, the inquirer enthusiastically replied, "Great, what did you learn?"

No parent ever complained to me about the outcome of our games, but I felt the pressure of their expectations. It was a performance standard I imposed on myself, but I held to the idea that winning wasn't the only benchmark of importance. When parents enrolled their children in soccer, they did it with the expectation that positive things would happen. However, "positive" can be defined in many ways.

Playing soccer is supposed to be fun, but every game is a contest with winners and losers. The puzzling question is: *If humans are gratified by winning, but half the players in every game don't receive that reward, how does a soccer coach motivate a struggling team to continue?*

My solution was to be honest with players and set goals we could accomplish. I also encouraged them to keep working and be resilient. I told them I was proud they kept battling when we fell behind during matches. I reminded them that nothing could be accomplished if we stopped playing, but if we kept working, we could "use the other team for practice" and improve our game. My intent was not to coerce them. I meant what I said because I wanted to win too, and I had to find something positive in every loss we experienced.

From my perspective, coaching was an odd contradiction. Coaching clinic instructors counseled me to deemphasize winning, then they taught me techniques that I could employ to defeat opponents. The competing emphases were confusing because some of the instructors were more eloquent than others, but the universal message was that I shouldn't sacrifice fairness and respect in pursuit of winning because encouraging players to work and do their best is rewarding regardless of the score. I agreed with that philosophy and practiced it. Yet, the paradox of coaching meant that a lack of parity existed between teams because every coach had a different idea of how much fairness could be sacrificed in pursuit of winning. Some let their urge to win hijack their sense of right and wrong and sought success at any cost without regard to fairness or the safety of others. Other coaches, like me, were less competitive. We didn't coach because we dreamed of guiding our children's team to regional championships. We participated because our children's teams needed coaches. We thought we had adequate soccer experience to do the job well—or, in my case, we had endured an ordeal that showed us that despite our limited knowledge, we could do the job better than some others.

When I became the leader of Wade's soccer team, I suspected the obligation would be mine for many years. I knew that the more time I spent with the team, the more significant my role as a mentor became because, to be effective, I encouraged other things besides soccer. Things like leadership, self-control, fairness, and the rewards of hard work. Those important lessons prepared players to compete and succeed in life beyond the game.

Chapter 22

The Giants

PLAYING SOCCER IN a rural area was a challenge. Towns competed against neighboring communities, and drive times for games ranged from ten to forty-five minutes. For families with players on different teams, game days were hectic. Players carpooled, coaches ferried those who didn't have rides, and parents divided and conquered to get players to games. After a season or two, the complex process became routine; after years, the routine became ritual.

On road trips, I looked forward to my favorite scenic overlook and visiting strategically located drive-ins on the way home for ice cream or lunch. The teams that we played became familiar as well. We saw the same ones every spring and fall, sometimes twice during seasons that lacked enough participants to fill the schedule.

Wade's team called our fourth opponent that fall, the Giants. They had two blond twin boys who towered over every other player on the field, standing at least a head taller. It looked unfair, as if our second graders were playing sixth graders. The first time we played, there was a moment before kickoff when both teams were in position on the field, waiting for the referee to start the game. There was a lull, an expectant pause when even the cheering parents fell silent. Players in brightly colored uniforms decorated the green field, and the sun peeked in and out of a mostly cloudy sky. It was a perfect soccer panorama, except for two tall, towheaded discontinuities.

I stood on the sideline, flanked on both sides by players. Some fiddled with their gear or a ball, and some, like me, looked on, struggling to process the magnitude of the challenge before us, contemplating what to do, wondering how good the two tall players were. Then, just before the first foot struck the ball, one kid uttered the word that summed it all up: "Wow." That was all I heard. A second later, the ball was in play, and I was coaching, reminding players to get back on defense when the other team had the ball, or trying to help them figure out how to deliver a throw-in when they lacked the physical strength to launch it over their opponent's head. My efforts didn't influence the outcome of the game much. Unlike our tall players, who were a little clumsy, the twins were physically well-coordinated and attacked and played together. We didn't have the skills to stop them. It was a demoralizing defeat, something like 6-0.

As we shook hands after the game, their coach sheepishly apologized. It was sincere, quick, and polite, "Good game, sorry about the score." I thought it was odd—no coach had ever apologized to me for winning. We didn't stop to chat. Instead, I headed back to the sideline and started collecting soccer equipment. Judy joined me after crossing the field from the parents' side. She smiled and said, "Rough game, huh?" Then she told me she had recognized a mom from the other team, a high school friend. The two enjoyed a wonderful conversation and got reacquainted. Judy learned that the woman's husband was the opposing team's coach, and the tall players were their offspring. The twins had struggled developmentally, which led to their parents' decision to hold them back from school for a year. Human growth and development being what it is, the twins caught up by the time we encountered them, but their Soccer Club allowed them to remain with their school cohort instead of reassigning them to an age-appropriate team.

Knowing something about the circumstances of our loss that day lessened its sting—parents had acted in their children's best interests. They made decisions years in advance that were reflected by the day's events. It wasn't fair to our team, but from the twins' perspective, I understood the desire to play soccer with friends. Life's not fair. The twins' parents probably thought that when faced with the daunting task of providing for two undersized newborn babies.

At the next practice, I told the Bulldogs not to worry about the score but to take the loss as a challenge: if we all worked to improve, we could beat a team that relied heavily on just two players. My monologue had the desired effect; it motivated players, and we kept practicing. The day that I predicted did finally come. It wasn't the next occasion we faced the Giants or the time after. It's been said that losing builds character—we had our share before the Giants fell, but the win was much sweeter for it.

WE ENDED OUR first fall season with two wins—just enough to know how it felt. Judy and I agreed that a celebration was in order, and we followed our typical order of ceremony. After the last game, I asked parents to assemble for a player recognition ceremony and team picture. I made a short speech thanking players and parents, called each player out onto the field, shook their hands, and gave them a small trophy. Then, I assembled the team in front of a goal while parents snapped team pics. After that, my job was done, but the party wasn't over. Some moms provided drinks and cookies decorated like soccer balls, and I was awarded a $100 gift card from a local sporting goods store. It was a nice gesture, and I appreciated it. Those parents loved me, which was a relief. I took their actions as a vote of confidence—we would do it again in the spring.

Chapter 23

Coaching Can Be a Thankless Job

OWEN'S SEASON-ENDING GAME was later that day. Judy and I joined most of the parents and sat on ridiculously small park bleachers; other spectators spread out along the sideline on collapsible chairs. The coaching dads, who were too restless to sit, stood near the sideline. Owen's team did not win, but he didn't care—he was having fun. His coaches, Henry and Felix, did not demean him or the team, which was a vast improvement. As the star defender, Owen teamed up with other players to move the ball and produce goals. His job was to destroy opposing attacks before they got organized, and he took his role seriously; few escaped with the ball. His position was in the middle third of the field, so he rarely scored, but that didn't matter. Owen enjoyed challenging, then winning the ball, and accelerating away. When defenders started to converge, he passed the ball to the forwards so they could take their best shot. Watching that process was fun because I knew from experience what would happen and could see the pieces come together.

At the end of the game, the coaches called the team and parents together on the field. As we joined the team, I grew concerned. Neither Judy nor I had heard anything about a coach thank-you gift. As Coach Henry began to speak, I scanned the parents for any hint that a gift was forthcoming. Henry's speech was like mine, except it didn't involve picture-taking or trophies. There was a long, awkward pause when he finished talking; seconds ticked by. It was a quiet afternoon in October; not even the crickets chirped. That would have been the perfect time for someone in the group to thank Henry and Felix and give them at least a handshake, but no one did. Those two dads had coached the team since kindergarten, five years, every fall and spring. It was a small town, everyone knew everyone else, and still, no one had taken the time to do anything. I felt bad because Henry's younger son was on my team, and we had enjoyed a grand celebration. Henry and Felix directed the team to a winning season, and they did a good job. They deserved something. To this day, I regret that I did not simply shout "Thank you" and lead a round of applause, but my newcomer status inhibited me. Fortunately, awkward moments don't last forever; Henry excused us, and the group broke up. Judy and I thanked both coaches before we left—a few other parents did the same.

That experience taught me that coaching would be more demanding than I imagined. Unforeseen things were going to happen that would be awkward and difficult. In addition to managing all the problems associated with young players, I was going to confront things that would challenge the expertise of most mental health professionals—things like angry parents and coaches who put winning before all else—and I would solve those problems in real-time with on-the-spot decisions. If I were successful, my reward would not be in the form of thank-you gifts or praise from parents—although those things made me feel more valued. Instead, my compensation and corresponding motivation for taking on the task stemmed from my experience with Coach Tom, which had taught me that there was only one thing more difficult than training my child's soccer team—enduring a bad coach training my child's soccer team.

Chapter 24

Trophy Ban

BY SPRING, WORD had gotten out about the trophies we awarded Wade's team. I never imagined an $8 plastic shooting star with a soccer ball sticker at its center, mounted atop a little piece of polished marble, would create a problem, but it did. No one contacted me directly. Instead, it came up at the spring coaches' meeting.

About halfway through the meeting, I noticed tension in the room. The club president avoided eye contact with the audience, especially me. She awkwardly craned her neck to address soccer board members sitting beside her in the front of the room while making vague, off-handed remarks about trophies. I listened, confused at first, then became concerned that I was the focus of the discussion. Eventually, she mustered the courage to address the audience.

"We don't award trophies," she said. "Trophies are for tournaments and the teams that win them."

Some soccer board members nodded in agreement.

No one mentioned me by name, perhaps because I was not the only guilty party. I didn't say anything. I was still new to the club, and I didn't think I had the political clout to put up a fight. I also didn't believe anyone wanted to know my position or would be swayed by it. Their minds were made up, but they did not understand what I was trying to convey. They followed a tradition where winning was the only thing that deserved special recognition. My motivation was different from theirs. I intended to reward effort, personal best, and teamwork because those things deserved recognition too. Unlike some participants in the discussion, I didn't believe that awarding trophies to Wade and his teammates gave a false impression that they had won every game. Players knew I was rewarding hard work and determination because I encouraged them often and mentioned it *right before* I handed them their trophies. I was never sure what was most upsetting to those soccer zealots. Were they upset about the diminution of the sanctity of winning, or were they upset that if their children were going to get a trophy, they would have to collect money, order trophies, and distribute them? I thought the latter after the awkward way Owen's season had ended with nothing for players or coaches.

TWO WEEKS LATER, we had our first spring practice. Players and parents must have been saying good things over the winter because our ranks grew from twelve to fourteen. Many soccer clubs would not have allowed our roster to get that large because we played 5v5, and there was not enough playing time for everyone. Most clubs would have limited the team to ten individuals so each player could play half the game. Our club didn't consult me, and I lacked the experience to know any better—I just kept coaching who they assigned to the team.

Involving fourteen players in a game wasn't difficult; I cycled them onto the field, substituting when I could. I allowed every child the same playing time. I didn't have A and B teams, though many coaches did. One of the soccer zealots from our club openly advocated for it and advised me to do it.

"Yeah, I have my A-team and bench warmers," he said with a laugh. "You have to. It's the only way to get that win."

I didn't argue. He was offering a different perspective, and I wanted to consider it. Ultimately, I concluded that it was unfortunate that he wasn't as passionate about fairness as he was about winning.

Most weeks, the problem of having too many players was not an issue because there were always a few who did not attend games. We lived in a relatively affluent village. When Judy and I shopped for houses for our relocation, we also shopped for schools. She scoured information from our realtor, websites, and school principals. School quality didn't dominate our housing decision because we were limited by availability, but it played a part. Ultimately, we settled on a house on the edge of a growing neighborhood in a great school district. The district attracted many families to the community. The drawback was that taxes were higher. Doctors, lawyers, and professionals with better-than-average salaries were the people moving to the area. Their children were involved in extracurricular activities that all seemed to happen on Saturdays. Dance, forensics, piano, gymnastics, riding class, and weekends in Chicago all whittled down my soccer roster. Often, I never knew how many players would attend until I saw who showed up on game day. Then I took a head count, consulted my pocket notebook, made a few adjustments, and played what we had. During games, I substituted players when I could. If someone got tired or hurt, I sent in kids who wanted more time.

IT WAS CHALLENGING to start practicing during spring in the Midwest, where March was often unpleasant. If the ground wasn't frozen, then it was wet and squishy. The only thing that dried it out was a chilly breeze. I usually started practice two weeks before the first game, and we practiced twice weekly, which offered four potential opportunities to familiarize players with what they were supposed to do and get rusty skills back up to snuff. Bad weather often canceled practices, and players frequently had conflicts due to their out-of-town spring break plans. I expected that if we tried on four occasions, everyone could manage to attend at least two before the first game. It didn't always work. Sometimes, Wade and I were the only ones to show up on blustery days, and some years, we managed only one practice before the first game.

Bad weather was not an excuse to miss practice. I tried to teach players to prepare for inclement weather. Many seven-year-olds are lean, without enough body fat to keep them warm in a gray, cold, windy drizzle. I didn't want a rainy game to be the first time they thought about what was needed to stay warm and dry. I encouraged them to wear layers: sweatshirt, sweatpants, raincoat, knit hat, and gloves or mittens, topped off with their jersey. I wanted them to plan for adversity because the league had an unusual standard of playing games in any weather. Referees were instructed, "Get the game out of the way. Don't cancel, no matter what." The dictum was hard on the fields when a downpour was in the forecast.

Wade and a core group of players embraced what I taught, came to practice routinely, and took it seriously. They didn't monkey around like some players on Owen's team. They followed me but behaved like leaders and provided a critical mass that made the rest of the team conform. I was grateful for their help.

Chapter 25

Little Victories

EFFECTIVELY KICKING A ball can be challenging. Anyone who has played kickball knows there are many ways to fail. Novice players often kick too early and miss the ball completely. Sometimes, they clumsily stub the toe of their kicking foot and stumble over the ball. Or they kick the ball but strike too late with the top of their foot, producing a pop-up. Very few kickball players manage a well-timed in-step kick and a home run. Learning to kick a stationary ball requires developing spatial awareness, proper form, and timing. It's more difficult to kick a moving ball and even more challenging for a running person to strike a rolling ball. Nevertheless, with sufficient practice, soccer players master it all, almost without thinking.

As our season progressed, I taught kicking and passing on the run, shielding the ball, goalkeeping, challenging an attacker, and composure. I tried to coach in an organized fashion, emphasizing skill building, but each lesson was more like the proverbial throwing a plate of spaghetti at the wall—some players floundered, others learned quickly. One player, Ben, was aggressive and a quick learner. His eyes lit up when I introduced shielding to the team, a technique where players who possess the ball use their bodies to block opponents. Ben was the middle child of three brothers and was accustomed to fighting for everything. He made a lasting impression on me when we crossed paths at a churchyard playground where he had possession of the only functioning swing, and his siblings wanted it. They were on either side of him, punching his shoulders, and weren't holding back. I cringed at the thump of fists on flesh, but Ben never flinched. He sat with a satisfied smile, securely grasping the chains of the swing, holding tight while his brothers relentlessly pounded, trying to dislodge him.

Small and well-coordinated, Ben mastered shielding quickly. That week, during our game, he was penalized for it. The circumstances were not egregious, just unfortunate. Ben was involved in a one-on-one situation in the middle of the field. He had the ball, and an opposing player charged at him. Ben stepped in front and turned his back to the other player, who ran into him and rebounded off. Ben maintained control but didn't know what to do next. His opponent charged again; Ben moved his body to block—the same result. Clearly, I hadn't emphasized that while they were shielding, players should get their heads up and pass to a teammate. By the third assault and rebuff, I was directing players to move to Ben for a pass, but it was too late. Ben's defense was so good that it looked flagrant, almost as if he was taunting the other player, and the referee blew his whistle. He should have let the play continue. Ben wasn't doing anything wrong; a few more seconds and he would have learned how to escape. Penalty aside, Ben's demonstration taught our team more about shielding than I ever could.

Ben was easy to teach; other players were not. I never

let players dodge participation if they were struggling with a skill. They didn't have to master it but were required to keep trying. Most mastered the basics, especially if I worked with them for a few minutes. Then I made a point of congratulating them. I had to make the best of little victories because we were lucky to eke out a couple of wins. Somehow that was enough. Our morale was good, and everyone had fun at practices.

Wade was another bright spot. It was rewarding to watch him get stronger and more coordinated. He was still incredibly flexible. We began every practice by stretching—it was a waste of time for him. When players stretched, I joined them because I needed it. On more than one occasion, I glanced up from my labor to see Wade sitting with his leg behind his head and half the team distracted, trying to do the same—he was always leading. I told him that his flexibility and height meant he had to work harder to accomplish things that were easy for other players. I didn't want him to become frustrated with his lack of strength; I wanted him to take it as a challenge to overcome. He never said a word about it. He just kept playing hard with his friends.

I LEARNED SUBSTANTIALLY from watching Owen's team compete and occasionally fail. Despite their frequent successes, some of his teammates made the same glaring mistakes repeatedly. One was passing the ball across the middle of the field in front of their goal, which almost always gave the other team a scoring opportunity. It happened when the opposing team was attacking close to the goal. Owen's teammates would succeed in breaking up the attack and win control of the ball, but then panic because of the proximity of opponents and kick without thinking. If the kicker didn't have the composure to control the ball's direction, there was a good chance it was cleared in front of the goal instead of toward the sideline. Passing toward the sideline to a team-mate was the best choice. Week after week, I watched them make bad decisions and pass across the middle of the field. The adjustment was obvious, but Owen's teammates either lacked skill, or his coaches didn't recognize the weakness. I was determined that Wade's team would not make the same error, so I devoted a training session to solving the problem.

I set up a worst-case scenario for defenders where they were positioned in front of the goal and intercepted a shot from the field. As the ball rolled to them, an attacker (me) converged, following up on the shot to finish it. I was the pressure, light at first, then intense. I instructed players to stay calm and resist the urge to blast the ball back in the direction from where it came. Instead, I encouraged them to control the ball, shield it from me, turn to the sideline, kick it off the field, or pass to a waiting teammate. One by one, each defender took their turn. I varied the ball's direction and angle of attack to make the exercise more challenging. Waiting participants must have been paying attention because, with each turn, the success rate increased until the drill seemed unnecessary, but I didn't stop until everyone had an opportunity.

The last player was Alan. He was the fastest kid on the team, intelligent, and loved to play defense, but he tended to panic. He passed across the middle often and was the main reason I targeted the weakness. He frustrated me. He had the ability to do the right thing but lacked self-control. For him, it was a confidence-building day. I wasn't sure of the out-come. I hoped the exercise wouldn't end in tears because the only way he would achieve the skill was for me not to allow any excuses and help him gain the necessary confidence and composure. That meant failure was not an option. I couldn't let him say, "I can't do it," and then brush it off and move on. He had to stand on the field, compete against me, and execute the skill.

So, under the watchful eyes of a goalkeeper, Alan and I took positions on the field, and a teammate kicked the ball into play. I wanted Alan to succeed. I came in at about half speed following the ball, making it easy for him to turn away and clear the ball to the side, but as I approached, he pan-icked and reacted without thinking. As usual, he kicked the ball back in the direction from where it had originated. I was disappointed but didn't show it. As I coasted to a stop near Alan, he said, "I can't do it."

I was upbeat. "You can do it—you have the time and ability. Just control it and turn."

He was one of the smartest kids in his class; I tried to appeal to the analytical part of his brain. Another chance pro-duced the same outcome, but it was more evident that he had time to make a move. On the third occasion, I changed my angle of attack, partially blocking his opportunity to clear the ball from where it had come. Faced with my looming pres-ence, Alan paused with the ball, then turned his back to me and kicked it to the side.

"You got it," I said, "One more."

I upped the pressure and attacked from a direction that made his turn more difficult, but the bad habit was broken; he cleared the ball efficiently. Still not satisfied, I instructed him to keep possession of the ball and escape by dribbling to the sideline. I made conditions as demanding as possible and charged at him from the sideline where he needed to go, but I was the old, slow coach, and Alan was the quick-footed seven-year-old. He scampered away from me like the Roadrunner from the Coyote. The lesson was a success. I felt confident that our team had mastered something that eluded Owen's team even though they were two years older.

I wanted to hammer home one more thing to avoid backsliding. I assembled the team and told them that to ensure we didn't forget the tactic, I would reinforce it periodically by shouting like a drill sergeant, "Never pass the ball across the field while defending your goal. Do you understand me?"

They were to respond with the sir sandwich, "Sir, yes sir."

My instructions were met with nervous side-eyeing. I didn't care; I needed a tool to emphasize the importance of what we learned. For the second time that day, I made players do something they didn't want to do. Their first response was weak; I made them do it again. The second time was louder, more fearless, and seemed to embody a change in attitude—a hint of a common bond.

The sir sandwich was a fun and valuable tool. Every time we performed it, the team grew bolder. It bound us together but wasn't enough to overcome our weaknesses. Every Saturday, we played a game that revealed a vulnerability; every Tuesday and Thursday, I solved a problem. That was how it went week after week. We played the Giants; they beat us again. As the weather got warmer, we celebrated Gator Day at our last practice and won our last game. There were no trophies afterward, but we had a grand cookie party, and I got another gift certificate for my efforts.

Chapter 26

Soccer Medallions

OUR SOCCER SEASON should have been complete, but it wasn't. Just at the end of the season, the Soccer Board announced that there would be a banquet on the Saturday following the last games. Everyone was supposed to attend: players, coaches, and parents. The venue was a local summer camp. After a season of many announcements, I sent home one more note explaining to parents what was going on, even though I didn't have many details. Families needed to RSVP so that the food requirement could be estimated. Neither the boys nor I wanted to go, but I felt that I had to attend since I was a coach. I told the boys they could be excused; nonetheless, they felt obligated to join me. So, on the first Saturday off after nine weeks of soccer, the boys and I drove to the summer camp. Judy stayed home with Megan.

The event was well attended. I parked relatively far from the venue because of the number of cars. As the boys and I walked to the dining hall, we stared in disbelief at anarchy on the grounds where dozens of unmanaged soccer players and their siblings swarmed. They were out of control on the climbing tower, hanging on swings, piled up on the slide, and running around like confused ants. There was no supervision,

and the novelty of a new playground had created an appall-
ing, almost unbelievable frenzy. Owen and Wade were as
shocked as I. Owen gaped at his teammates, who clung to the
over-taxed tower, competing for the highest perch. He wanted
to socialize with a friend but wasn't interested in ascending
what looked like a dangerous pinnacle of fools. Wade, who
disliked noise and crowds, wasn't tempted because his teammates were not on the playground. The three of us continued
to the dining hall, where Wade and I sat at a table colonized
by teammates, and Owen found his coaches.

As I chatted with players and parents, Dawn, the club
president, approached and handed me a small cardboard box
containing commemorative medallions. "These are for your
team," was all she said.

I was confused and a little irritated because she had ad-
monished me for awarding trophies. That interaction had
been embarrassing and weakly justified, but I complied out of
respect for her and the soccer organization. Her new instructions to reward players with medals felt like she was dropping
a hypocritical bomb in my lap—one for which I was not prepared because it required a presentation in a relatively formal
setting.

I mulled over the situation as Wade and I waited in line
for our bratwurst and potato salad. I was first in the lineup because I had the youngest team. What was I going to say? What
was I expected to say? The circumstance that concerned me
most was that I hadn't brought a roster of player names. I was
terrible at names, especially last names. I knew my players by
their first names. The harder I tried to remember last names,
the faster they vaporized from my memory.

Wade and I finished our meal, bussed our trays, and sat

down as Dawn began to address the group. She explained that the soccer banquet was a new idea, and the event was the first of what would be a new tradition. I listened, hoping she didn't credit the Beers Trophy Incident as the impetus for the event. I had difficulty concentrating on her words because I was trying to recall last names. Her speech was brief, and then, without pausing, she introduced me.

I rose from my chair and called the team to join me on the stage. About half of the team attended the event. They lined up and waited for my instructions. My mind raced. I spoke the first words that popped into my head:

"Everyone tries to control their future. Sometimes, with hard work, they succeed. I'm proud of how hard this team worked. We began behind the skill curve last fall, practiced hard, and improved. Because of that effort, I think we can look forward to a better future."

As I finished, I looked out at the audience. They looked at me silently, intently. Some were beaming and looked on the verge of tears, as if my words had touched them deeply. Then I turned to the team and thought again about those elusive names. I could only remember one besides Wade's. I announced that player's first and last name, shook their hand, and awarded a medallion. Then I looked back at the rest of the team, queued in line, waiting. The first was William— Williammm … who? I paused with his medallion in my hand, thinking as hard as I could, hoping that his last name would come to me, feeling myself blush with embarrassment and frustration. The clock ticked. I glimpsed at the audience, which was still aglow, watching, anticipating more inspiring words or perhaps just the first and last name of the next medallion receiver.

I swallowed hard and looked back at William, who waited patiently, a smiling little mass of bones and muscle. He looked at me sympathetically as if to say, *Come on, Coach, you can do it*.

Finally, I thought, *He is probably nervous in front of this crowd. Just give him the medal.* My presentation was getting more awkward with each passing moment. As my anxiety grew, even first names were starting to slip away. Finally, I gave up and blurted "WILLIAM" into the microphone. He strode across the stage, collected his medallion, and we shook hands. It went the same way for the rest of the team.

I handed out generic soccer medallions to the fraction of the team who attended the banquet in front of what was, to them, a bunch of strangers. At the end, the whole room clapped for us. Yet, somehow, it did not seem as rewarding as our simple trophy ceremony where there was no crowd, and the applause was from parents for their children—the homemade cookie was sweeter, the lukewarm juice box more satisfying.

I know that members of the Soccer Board had their hearts in the right place about awards. They wanted to ensure that no one was left out and everyone was treated equally. Unfortunately, their agenda failed because of competing interests and a lack of agreement between the board and everyone else. That is why only a fraction of our team attended the banquet, and I went home with a stack of unawarded medallions.

There was a formality that existed in our corner of the Midwest that was uncommon in our previous home. In the fast-growing, somewhat liberal university town, people referred to each other by their first names; in our new home, it was always Mr. Beers. Even adults referred to each other that way. Soccer zealots embraced the formality. Rules existed for the sake of rules, and meetings were held because we had to have them, not because we needed them. Once convened, many meetings turned into social events led by a few attention-starved individuals who held everyone else captive.

I didn't have time for socializing because I was a parent with three kids and the spouse of a psychologist who worked evenings. My typical workday was action-packed: arrive at work at 6:30 a.m., work until 4:00 p.m., get Megan from daycare if it was my turn, make her a snack, go to soccer, go home, start homework, make dinner, eat dinner, finish homework, clean up dinner, sit down and do something with a kid, fall asleep sitting up, wake up, do the bedtime ritual which worked better on me than my kids, wake up again, do something else, go to bed. Of course, I didn't always do it alone. Judy helped, and when I was at work, she parented solo: urging sleepy children out of bed in the morning, making breakfast, packing lunches, rushing off to school or daycare, going to work, and doing all the other things that made our household well-organized and functional. With all that going on, soccer socializing wasn't a priority for either of us.

Chapter 27

Year 6–Player Passes

AUGUST CAME, AND with it, another fall coaches' meeting. I was starting to resent them because they were longer than necessary and were dominated by soccer zealots with whom I often found myself at odds. The meetings were one of the things that made coaching feel like a chore instead of an opportunity. Despite reservations, I knew the meetings were necessary. They provided an occasion to update coaches and distribute rosters and equipment. They also indoctrinated new coaches. A confident few of them had prior experience; most were overwhelmed. I identified first-time coaches by their perplexed expressions as they churned through their newly acquired gear bags filled with balls, cones, pinnies, and first-aid supplies. They were as clueless as I was at Owen's first soccer practice. No one explained what was expected of them or how to get help. Like me, most coaches would have offered suggestions if they sought guidance. We would have helped, even though we jealously allocated free time because of other obligations.

I was relieved not to be the new guy anymore. As the meeting proceeded, I listened to the organizational material and studied my new roster. There was turnover on the team, with three players departing and three enlisting. However, the team was a little more manageable because we advanced to a larger field and 6v6 player format.

After about forty minutes, the club president finished her presentation and opened the meeting for questions. I felt a wave of relief because there was no mention of the Beers Trophy Incident; apparently, that breach of protocol was forgiven. When the meeting broke down into individual problem-solving, I took my equipment and headed home. It was still early and there was time to notify players when practice would begin.

THE FOLLOWING WEEK, we started again with another first practice/team meeting to introduce players and educate parents. From the standpoint of personnel, player turnover was a wash—we lost two girls and a boy and gained the same. From the standpoint of boots on the ground, there was a vast improvement because we gained two coaches. Neither had played soccer, but coaches Charlotte and Pete were athletic and enthusiastic. We were a good match and became friends. Coach Charlotte helped at practices, and Pete helped at games.

A regimen of pregame practices refreshed the team's basic skills and introduced our new players to the standard code of conduct, the sir sandwich, in response to "Never pass the ball across the field while defending your goal." I also spent time with our goalkeepers.

We had four players who wanted to be goalkeeper—that was unusual. Many teams struggled because no one wanted the job. Being a goalkeeper put players on the spot. All eyes were on them when it was attacker versus goalkeeper. On occasions when multiple attackers surrounded our goal, it could be a battle with kicked soccer balls ricocheting off posts or players before being kicked again—all in seconds. The goalkeeper stood like a single combatant surrounded, defending a prize. Sometimes, the keeper captured the ball with a dramatic thud; other times, the attacker's first shot was lethal, so well-placed that the keeper hadn't a chance.

Expecting eight-year-old goalkeepers to behave like the professional players on TV wasn't realistic. Those professionals throw themselves at the ball. They read their opponent's body language to anticipate where the ball will be kicked, then lunge. That level of play requires years of practice. I worked with players who were there for fun. Something about goalkeeping appealed to them. To succeed, our players needed a "nose for the ball." They all had it, especially Wade. He had a knack for anticipating where an attacking player was going and somehow got to that spot before the ball arrived. I don't know how he did it because he wasn't particularly speedy; his low muscle tone robbed him of that. Nevertheless, he was prescient and instinctively cut off attackers before they could kick.

To encourage our keepers, I learned about goalkeeping and prioritized what I could teach during the minutes we had at practices. I taught the ready position so that hands were up and players could react quickly to the ball. I told them where to stand so the ball's momentum would not carry them into the goal. Keepers are the only players on the field permitted to touch the ball with their hands. That warranted special attention. I instructed them to pair up and roll, kick, and throw balls to each other until they learned to capture a ball instinctively in a basket of their arms and hands. Each week, I introduced new skills and then handed the drills off to Coach Charlotte to administer the repetitions. Lastly, I told them that goalkeeping was a tough job—goals would get scored, and they shouldn't take it personally, as if it were their fault.

Each keeper had their own style of play. Consequently, it was difficult for me to judge if what I taught worked. I think I did instill confidence and give them a ritual of preparedness. They at least looked like goalkeepers when things got intense and knew what to do with the ball when they had it.

EVERY FALL BEFORE the first game, a flurry of phone calls and activity centered around player passes. When parents signed their child up for soccer, they had to provide a 1-by-1-inch picture for the player's identification card—the player pass. Player passes were printed on official Youth Soccer Association stationery and contained every player's name, birth date, and age group. Printing player passes was a tedious job. It likely fell to a person with the tech-savvy to accomplish the task of data entry and printing forms—probably the eleven-year-old child of the club registrar. Player passes were always done in a rush at the last minute because our club kept adding players to rosters until the first game. The club had an official registration deadline weeks before the first game, but parents either missed it or potential participants didn't decide until practices started. Then, there was a glut of parents calling to get their players on a team.

In the big city, the club registrar was relatively anonymous. Sticking to a deadline policy was easy for them, but not so in our small town. It was hard to say, "No, you missed the deadline. Your daughter cannot be enrolled at this time," to the woman who provided daycare for your child and was a close friend. Thus, even when the rosters were closed, they were open, and player passes were the last step. The process culminated with delivering player-pass construction materials to me, usually a day or two before the first game. I received an official registration document and picture for every player on the team. At the bottom of the form was a player membership card. I was required to detach each membership card and affix the picture (thermal lamination was preferred, but transparent tape was acceptable). Official procedure dictated that player passes be used with the roster to confirm each participant's identity before a game. The passes were supposed to be distributed to players before check-in, then the referee collected them as each individual was inspected. But in our rural league, the practice was relaxed, and there was no requirement that they be dispersed to players. The referees did not use them to confirm anything, yet before every game, I had to rummage through my gear bag and transfer the passes to the officials for the duration. It was an annoyance, especially on windy or rainy days.

I didn't have an issue with check-in because there had to be some effort to ensure that players on a team were legitimately registered, and the refs also used the time to examine each player's shoes and uniform. That made sense, but I wondered why I was required to construct the passes if they were never used for official purposes. The soccer zealots said the cards had to be present at every game. Occasionally, coaches admitted they didn't have passes—their confession to the referee was met with a stern look, a permissive shrug, and nothing more.

Referee training must have emphasized player-pass confirmation because they all asked for them. From my perspective, it was busy work. It was a rule enforced not for official purposes but because a rule existed and the responsibility for their construction could be delegated. They were intended to confirm a player's enrollment on a team, but they were never used for that purpose. They were redundant, superfluous, pointless—and required.

Chapter 28

The Purples

AS OUR FIRST game of the season approached, I was hopeful. Player for player, our skills were getting better. I couldn't help thinking that maybe this was our year—the year when we turned the corner to a winning season. We were improving, getting stronger, and doing the work. *Do the work, and you get rewarded with success.* That was how I thought at the beginning of the year, but the team was still untested. That test, the first game, revealed how the season would go.

We lost, beaten by a team we had not played before. It was not a blowout, but it was not close either. I tried to hide my disappointment, but Judy could see how I felt as she met me, and we walked off the field after the game. It was going to be another long season.

The following week was our introduction to a nightmare for the team and me. We played the Purples. They were a group of boys who were a year younger than Wade's team but were playing up, competing in our age bracket because they were a select team—players were hand-picked by the coach. That was possible because the Purples were from a larger soccer club with enough players to construct multiple teams in each age bracket. Their coach wanted to compete at a higher level, so he skimmed the best players and piled them all into one group. Pitting an all-boys select team against a coed rec team seemed wrong. The league had rules that prohibited the practice, but the Purples probably received a special dispensation because soccer zealots admired their lofty goal, and a select team elevated the status of the soccer program.

Unfortunately, there were no other elite teams in our area against which they could compete, so the Purples traveled often and reached an agreement with our soccer league. Consequently, we faced them on the second Saturday of the season and for years to come.

The Purples' coach knew soccer well. He was short and fit and moved with determination. As they played, he barked perfectly timed commands to each player: challenge, pressure, stop, turn, TJ is open, pass, shot. He called the entire game that way. They played like a well-oiled machine—a machine with speedy little parts that zoomed around and blitzkrieged us. There was nothing fair about it, no point in sugarcoating it; our butts got mercilessly kicked. At the end, my head was spinning, and I wasn't playing. I could only imagine what Wade's teammates were thinking.

If there was a bright side to the experience, it was that I learned a few things about soccer tactics. Because the coach called the game so thoroughly, it was like he was coaching me. I could hear the call and then watch the player execute the move. There were lessons to be learned if I could swallow my pride and understand them. After the game, a mom, who must have sensed my disappointment, came to the sideline to tell me what she knew. She was acquainted with the parents of one of the opposing players, so she was aware of the select status and relayed it to me. She was trying to make me feel better. It didn't help. I was deeply disappointed—not for my-self, but for Wade and the team who had worked so hard, only to be destroyed by a group using us for practice so they could prepare to play tournaments and win trophies. It didn't seem right, and yet, it was allowed.

The following week at practice, I couldn't say much to make the team feel better, so I didn't dwell on the past. Instead, I did my homework. I flipped through my notes from soccer clinics and went to practice with some fun new drills that focused on our weaknesses. My effort was successful; there were no discussions or complaints about the game. We just moved on in preparation for the next match.

THAT WEEKEND WE were competitive but lost to anoth-er all-boys team—not a select team, just a coed team with no girls. It was an emerging pattern that confused me. I noticed a decreasing number of girls in our coed league each sea-son, and we faced more all-boys squads. The trend resulted from girls quitting or being diverted to their own division. Unfortunately, our club didn't have that option. Our soccer program was so small we barely had enough players to fill rosters by combining girls and boys.

The Giants were next. They defeated us, but at least they remained coed. We played well, and it was a close game; still, the losses aggravated me. I could sense the potential to win each time we played, but we had too many breakdowns. Part of it was my fault. I was still learning while trying to coach a game I had never played.

As our season ended, our hard work paid off. Wade and

the other tall boys grew into their long bones and got stronger, faster, and more coordinated. We managed to win two of three games. It was a relief, but not enough to wipe out my frustration with the Purples or the Giants. I knew our games would not get easier because the attrition of girls in the league would probably continue, and we would see more all-boy teams.

Chapter 29

Moving On

AFTER THE LAST game, I performed a routine ceremony. I called parents to our sideline then introduced
each player and shook their hand. Then I assembled the team
and coaches before a goal for pictures. We posed and smiled
while parents jostled for position to get a good photo or video.
As the flurry of shutter noises subsided, an idea occurred to
me. I asked the coaches to step out and the players to remain.

View screens flipped back open, and cameras whirred to
life in preparation for the demonstration. When the parents
looked ready, I turned to the team and shouted, "Never pass
the ball across the field while defending your goal. Do you
understand me?"

The team answered in perfect unison, booming, "SIR,
YES, SIR," as if they were Marines in bright soccer uniforms.
Most parents laughed, some looked shocked, and the team
was happy.

The digital record collected by those parents probably still exists. It's out there, unwatched, on obsolete digital media, sliding around the bottom of a drawer that only
gets used when someone needs an envelope or an old address

book. Parents try to capture special moments because they know their children will grow and move on.

Moving on was happening in our family. When we relocated to our new home, we put the boys in the same bedroom—they traditionally slept in bunk beds, and we kept the same setup. But a year had elapsed since the move, and Owen was in fifth grade. The demands of school were growing, and he often stayed up late on school nights doing homework. Wade still needed his sleep. So, we split the boys up, each to their own room, and on that day, the ritual of me saying good night to both of them at the same time ended.

For me, thresholds like that were meaningful. I couldn't stop them from happening. Most of the time, I didn't see them approaching. I passed through them and became aware that I was no longer doing what I took for granted. The bedtime tradition was special to me, and I was sad to experience its end. It started when Wade was about two and Owen was four. In those days, I tucked the boys in every night. They slept in bunk beds because that was our solution to persuade Owen to stay in his bed. He was a social animal, and sleeping alone was a problem for him, so Judy and I reasoned that if we put Wade in the same room with Owen, we all might get a better night's sleep. The plan worked. Owen slept in the top bunk and Wade on the bottom. Some nights, I tucked them in simply with a quick hug; other nights, we shared a story. On those occasions, I sat beside Wade and read a book everyone agreed on.

Sometimes, when we could not decide on a book, we created our own stories. That was how we conceived the adventures of Fartle. Fartle was a large, flatulent bull who liked to go exploring. We invented all sorts of stories: Fartle

Eats the Christmas Tree, Fartle Explores a Spooky Cave, and Fartle Fights a Dragon. They all ended the same way: a sizeable gaseous explosion and a scorched Fartle limping back to his favorite hilltop to munch some tasty grass. Judy never told Fartle stories, but she knew about them. She marveled that in fiction and life, there was always a flatulent bull.

Andy's Advice ... for Players

This book is peppered with advice for coaches and parents, but players are the stars of recreational soccer. They have a share in the responsibility to make their team successful, and within them reside future soccer parents and coaches. So here are ten recommendations for the youngest among us. Players, coaches, and parents who embrace this guidance will foster a better soccer experience for all.

1. **Soccer is supposed to be fun.** Like most things in life, the rewards of soccer depend on how much effort is invested. Don't be so involved in the pursuit of winning that you forget that soccer is just a game. Winning is not the only enjoyable aspect of the sport: shutting down an opposing player, making a well-timed pass to a teammate, collecting the ball for a save, and achieving a personal best can all be rewarding regardless of a game's outcome. Win or lose, find what's fun.

2. **Attend practices** because team weaknesses are corrected and new skills are introduced continuously. You need to be present to keep pace with your teammates.

3. **Practice with enthusiasm.** Team practices are not busy work; there are good reasons for all the activities. Running increases endurance; repetitions of toe taps build muscle memory so you can control the ball by touch and keep your eyes up; drills with your weak foot increase agility with the ball so you can turn left or right; and pushups build upper-body strength so you can recover quickly after a fall.

4. **Push yourself during training**—don't be afraid to make a mistake. Nothing bad happens if you make an error during practice.

5. **Let the coach be the coach.** If you have a complaint about another player, relay your concerns and let the coach handle the situation. Your responsibility is to play soccer.

6. **Keep your composure.** Getting flustered doesn't help you meet your obligation to the team.

7. **Always put forth your best effort**—don't give up. When you lose the first half of a game, brush it off and try to win the second half. If you can win the second half, you might win the game.

8. **Play fair,** or you will lose the respect of opponents and friends.

9. **Shake hands with your opponent.** Regardless of how good or bad you feel after the game, put the competitiveness of the contest behind you.

10. **Work to improve.** You may not always get what you want, but with effort and practice, you will become a better soccer player.

Chapter 30

Giants Fall

WINTERS WERE LONG in the upper Midwest. The first significant snowfall was met with excitement, but as the days went by, I got tired of shoveling, and Judy grew weary of hanging up wet snow pants. Basketball season started for Owen, and then there was Christmas and more basketball. In our house, February brought Megan's birthday. February could be brutal, so any excuse for a party was welcome. Unfortunately, the afterglow didn't last long, and cabin fever set in—kids went nuts. By March, there was a hint of spring in the air, chickadees started to sing, and crocuses sprouted from the lawn to be gobbled up by hungry deer. That was when our Soccer Club scheduled the spring meeting, and I started thinking about the upcoming season.

Once again, I listened respectfully to the requisite lecture and perused my updated roster. We lost a player but gained a player. Our numbers were the same—nine boys and five girls. That was good news. One new player meant that a deep dive into fundamental training wouldn't be required; instead, we could build on what we had. The annual cycle of meetings, practices, and games had become routine. I had everything dialed in. I knew where all the soccer fields were and how to direct our team's parents to those locations. I had templates for administrative tasks, and my assistant coaches knew their respective roles. I kept notes from the previous season to remember where we left off and what aspects of our game needed more work. My practices were fast-paced and efficient. Despite the business-like atmosphere and the sir-sandwich rejoinders, I was not an authoritarian coach. I treated players like adults and appealed to their common sense. I was lucky. Most players were respectful and well-behaved. They gave their best effort if I explained what we were doing and why.

Our season went quickly. We won two games, and in a magnificent turn of events, one was against the Giants. It wasn't a spectacular victory—we didn't magically master an aspect of the game that had escaped us. We played our game, stopped the twins with tenacious defense, and came out on top. Afterward, during the handshake, I followed the team, listening to each player offer a respectful "Good game" until I stood face-to-face with the Giants coach. For an instant, we paused like we were old friends. I changed my form from a high-five to a formal handshake and offered it. We shook hands, and then, with a bewildered expression, he said, "How'd you do that?" I almost thought I would never hear those words from his mouth. I had told our team for nearly two years that they could beat the Giants if they kept working, and we had done it. I had no answer for him. Nothing extraordinary came to mind.

"We just kept working," I said.

We both smiled and then went back to our teams. Judy, Megan, Owen, and a few other parents joined our team as we packed up. We lingered for a while, savoring the moment. We had played enough soccer to know it was essential to enjoy our victories because there was no way of knowing when we would experience another. That was sound wisdom because we never played the Giants again.

ANOTHER VICTORY THAT season was memorable because Wade scored his first goal. We played at a Veterans' Memorial Park decorated with a decommissioned tank. It was a cold, gray spring day, and as the game progressed, it started to sprinkle. Our team was well prepared for the weather. Coach Pete managed players on our sideline, dividing his efforts between tying shoestrings for players with fingers too cold to function and helping them hang on to the blanket they used for a makeshift tent in the windy conditions.

The circumstances leading up to Wade's goal reflected our improved defense and teamwork. I watched as we fought off an attack, fended it to the side, and transitioned from defending to counterattacking. Wade waited at midfield as the team moved the ball up the sideline away from our goal. He played forward and loitered, unguarded, in open space. I had encouraged the team to come prepared for chilly weather; on that day, it looked as if they wore everything they owned. Hats, gloves, mittens, hooded sweatshirts, and sweatpants were worn under their uniforms, making the ordinarily lean bunch of soccer players appear unusually bulky. I found it difficult to coach because I struggled to identify players— but I knew Wade. He wore a blue stocking cap and a long-sleeved gray sweatshirt underneath his uniform. I watched as a well-insulated teammate passed him the ball. He trapped it, then quickly turned and got moving. He dribbled past midfield, picking up speed and angling toward the goal as opposing players moved to challenge.

The last third of the field remained when an opponent stepped in and tried to stop him. Wade didn't slow but made a quick move and was past the player instantly. A few more steps, and he kicked a hard, line-drive ball on the ground. I watched in anticipation as the ball rolled past a numb goalkeeper into the back of the net. A cheer went up from our parents.

For me, it was the culmination of years of effort. Judy and I encouraged our children to play sports because we thought it was good for them. It got them off the couch and made them physically fit. I coached because I wanted Wade to have a positive and fun experience. I knew that if he was going to play in high school, he needed something to motivate him to build the strength and endurance required to succeed at that level. The event affirmed that our plan was working for Wade because he was getting stronger, faster, more coordinated, and had the physical strength to push past other players.

As I watched him walk back to midfield to restart the game, I wanted to run out and congratulate him, but the referee would have objected. I shouted his name loud enough that I knew he would hear me. He acknowledged with a *big* smile while collecting high-fives from teammates. It was another meaningful lifetime moment.

Chapter 31

Girls and Boys Are Not the Same

IDIDN'T KNOW IT then, but that was our Golden Season. On a team-by-team basis, we were the most competitive that we would ever be. The following fall, our players were nine years old and in the fourth grade. It was a convention in most of the surrounding soccer clubs to divide their boys and girls into different leagues at that stage. Boys played coed, and girls played in their division. Our small community did not have enough players to do that. There was no girls' team for our five to join.

The birth of my daughter solidified my status as a feminist. I wanted my daughter to receive the same pay as her male counterparts and for her successes and failures to be judged on the same criteria as a man. However, I did not believe that girls and boys were physically equal. Most males have testicles, and the hormones produced by those glands make the average boy larger and stronger than the average girl. It didn't matter that some of our girls were more capable than some of the boys; what mattered was that we fell behind in average ability, and those testicles tipped the scales when we competed against an all-boys team. The boys were getting faster, stronger, and more aggressive than our girls.

There was nothing that I could do as a coach to offset that physical advantage, so I focused on improving my assigned players. I treated everyone the same during practices. I did not segregate them by gender during 1v1 drills, although I allowed them to pair up if they wanted to. Similarly, during games, assignments were based on my practice of rotating players through various positions. Each player had strengths and weaknesses. I did my best with the resources that were available.

THE SEASON ENDED with a second annual soccer banquet. I learned from my mistakes and took a roster of player names. We weren't the youngest team anymore—some other coach had to sweat going first. When it was my turn, I didn't have many heartwarming words. I wasn't a fan of the banquet and didn't want to bolster support, so I kept my speech simple and announced each player's number and name while handing out medallions.

The banquet was less well attended than the first and was also the last. The soccer zealots must have determined that there was no need for it. The rebellion that the Beers Trophy Incident started had been suppressed.

There was no official policy to deal with the occasional awkwardness associated with the reality that some coaches had a celebration at the end of a season, and others didn't. I adopted a "Don't ask, don't tell, don't award trophies" approach. At the end of a season, I contributed a brief recognition ceremony, handshake, and an opportunity for a team pic. A few moms were always willing to organize a celebration with cookies, cake, and, occasionally, pizza after the last game. No one objected to that.

Still, I thought the soccer board should have been less concerned with the nature of awards at our cookie party and more engaged with club organization, information transfer to coaches, and encouraging sportsmanship. Too many board members replaced an emphasis on sportsmanship with competitiveness. That substitution meant that they were less concerned with fairness and fun. Within a team, that attitude meant weak players were relegated to the bench until they lost interest and quit, a pattern reflected by dwindling player numbers as teams advanced to older ages. Purging weak players decreased parity between teams as large squads became increasingly above average in skill compared to small ones that fielded all players equally out of necessity. The trend increased the disparity between teams, producing lopsided victories and callous behavior.

Chapter 32

Year 7–Death in the Family

MY DAD PASSED away in August, just before our first fall game. I wasn't especially close to him. My move to attend graduate school put distance between us in more than one way. He had a traditional view of his role as a parent and breadwinner for the family. I doubt he ever changed my diaper when I was a baby, and he showed little interest in coaching or supporting the athletic teams on which I played. He wasn't particularly involved as a grandparent, either. He liked his grandchildren, but his spare time was filled with hobbies. I don't think he saw Owen or Wade play a soccer game. I wasn't devastated by his death, but it was a shock because he died suddenly. He was my father, not my close father. I shed a few tears, spoke at his funeral, and our family moved on.

The co-occurrence of his death with the ramping up of fall soccer made for a hectic agenda—too hectic for some things related to soccer. One of those things, player passes, began a chain of events that illustrated one of the disappointing aspects of coach-parent interactions.

The death of a friend or relative often leads to a reevaluation of personal priorities. I handled the loss of my dad well, but the construction of player passes was too much for me. I couldn't bring myself to do it. It was trivial, and I had other things to do that were more important. I wanted to delegate the task to the parents because they often offered that if I ever needed help, all I had to do was ask. It was a simple task, and I didn't want to overthink it. I planned to hand the job to the first parent I saw at the next practice.

Unfortunately, the first parent I saw was the lioness from the first-ever day of practice. She refused my request and lectured, "I don't have time for that. The time when Alan is at practice is my time." I stood in silence, with the bag of player pass construction materials in my hand, thinking that the benefits of my time-saving solution were vanishing with every word and second that ticked by.

I waited until she finished, then started looking for the next parent. Telling the lioness I was asking because I had recently buried my dad didn't seem appropriate, although it probably would have worked. My search was short; the next parent accepted the task gladly.

That lioness lecture made an impression on me. I felt insulted. I wanted to say something but chose not to because F-bomb phrases were on my tongue. Her refusal was offensive for two reasons. First, her words and attitude belittled my efforts as a volunteer coach. I contributed much more than free babysitting, which was how she seemed to regard it. Second, her response presumed that others could afford the time to construct the passes, but she couldn't. I couldn't understand how she rationalized that her free time was more valuable than mine or anyone else's.

MY DAD'S DEATH ultimately led to a happy adventure for Owen, Wade, and me. He and I shared an interest in fishing and made a tradition of going on annual outings. I tried to rekindle that practice with him and the boys but was mostly unsuccessful. When he passed, his boat was stranded in storage "up north." To retrieve it, the boys and I did something we had never done before. We excused ourselves from Saturday soccer games and drove north on a chilly but clear October weekend. When we arrived, we paid his storage bill, checked out the boat, then went fishing. I did my best to find his favorite spots, and on the second day, we caught a respectable bunch of walleye and perch. I commemorated the day by snapping a picture of two happy boys dressed in their brightly colored red and yellow winter jackets, holding a stringer of fish between them against a backdrop of the boat and an intense, blue autumn sky. It was the kind of experience that I shared with my dad on a few occasions—he would have enjoyed it.

Chapter 33

Channeling Zeno of Citium

FACED WITH THE challenges of managing a struggling team, I tried to increase the odds of success by equipping myself with soccer knowledge. I went to coaching clinics every summer and sometimes winter. They helped me better understand the game, and I began appreciating the subtleties of drills and tactics. I also watched soccer on TV, studied it on the internet, and went to Owen's games and practices to preview the future of Wade's team. Despite my investment, our victories dwindled to about one each season, and the recurring nightmares continued. The Purples humiliated us every spring and fall, and we were increasingly more likely to suffer an embarrassing loss to every all-boys team we encountered.

It was difficult for the team and me to lose that many games. But, if I was honest, nothing I could say could sugarcoat a bitter defeat and make the sting of another loss go away. So, I stuck to my script. "Forget about the score. I don't care about the score. The point is to have fun and improve." There were instances of individual brilliance and teamwork when it was fun. Personal-best moments became the highlight reel in my head. Unfortunately, with few exceptions, highlights were all there was, and it remained unlikely that conditions would change.

Merriam-Webster's Dictionary defines the word "Stoic" as *a member of a school of philosophy founded by Zeno of Citium about 300 B.C.* There is more: *Stoics accept what happens in their lives without complaining or showing emotion.* Stoic describes what we became. We celebrated when we won a game, but the festivities were tempered by knowing how it felt to be the other team. Wins were an opportunity for encouragement and a reward for hours of practice. When we lost a game, we moved on—no player pointed a finger or cried. Stoicism was our psychological fortress. Had I known that I was teaching the philosophy of Zeno of Citium, I think I would have asked for more compensation than a cookie at the end of the season.

Chapter 34

Owen's Team Dwindles

WHEN OWEN GRADUATED to the seventh grade, he and his soccer team advanced to a larger field and full-scale 11v11 player format. That's when his team began to struggle because they didn't have enough players. It was the same small-community effect that haunted Wade's team. Interest in playing American football was luring players away. Additionally, B-team attrition pruned the roster as neglected players lost enthusiasm and quit.

That fall, when they encountered the problem for the first time, Owen's coaches tried to compensate by making a last-minute effort to drum up players. They called individuals who had been with the team in the past but hadn't registered, and they even tried to work out deals with players where they didn't need to attend practice, just games. Unfortunately, those attempts didn't work because prospective players either rejected the appeals or agreed to join the team but failed to make it official and register.

The misinformation led to a frustrating and disappointing season. Owen's team transformed from winning most of their games to being unable to field a team. When they didn't have enough players, opposing coaches varied in their responses. Competitive coaches argued that it wasn't fair to their players to suffer reduced playing time—they fielded eleven players versus our nine or ten. A sporting few loaned our team players so a game could proceed. Those coaches understood that there was no glory in beating a team that was short two players—that a victory, under those circumstances, was hollow because although they won without cheating, the contest wasn't fair.

I was frustrated because being short-handed at games was a relatively common occurrence. We weren't the only ones affected by it, but the league had no plan to deal with it. The soccer zealots at league headquarters scolded coaches who canceled a game because of a player shortage, but they had no policy to solve the problem. They desperately needed a solution because playing a game with one team understaffed was pointless. It was senseless for everyone to drive those miles and waste time playing a game that wasn't fair. The solution was obvious to me: an equal number of players should compete. If a team was short two players, instead of matching eleven against nine, both teams should field nine players. That would at least have offered a sporting challenge.

As an observer of Owen's games, I noticed that something happened when coaches shared players to provide an opportunity for a competitive scrimmage: it changed the flavor of the game. When teams were mixed, competitive parents didn't cheer or get frustrated. Coaches didn't feel compelled to win—often, they stopped coaching and just let the two teams play. I admit that when the teams were mixed, the resulting dynamic seemed to diminish the excitement of watching the game from a spectator's perspective. On those occasions, we achieved what the Dalai Lama would have espoused, "Play for the reward of playing," but it wasn't as fun as playing to win. Was it more fun than losing? Perhaps, but because we could not field a team, the referee marked the game report a forfeit, and everyone knew it. That stigma made it feel like a loss, no matter the outcome. A change in the philosophy of why we participated was required: "Play for fun" or "Play for personal best," as opposed to "Play to win."

When I was a child, my friends and I often met at a local vacant lot to play tackle football. It was unofficial and in-formal. There were no uniforms or lines on the field—just a bunch of kids who squared off and played. Everyone recognized a good play from a busted one and a touchdown from a turnover-on-downs. There were occasional arguments, but wins and losses didn't matter because the outcome and the teams vanished when players went home for dinner. We played for fun because no league or organization existed to record who won. Somehow, that spirit was lost within the organized framework of rec soccer. It was as if providing coaches and a referee corrupted the best part of the game.

The old coach who taught my first soccer clinic suggested it would be better if parents dropped their kids at a game and went away until it ended. Maybe he should have gone further and encouraged all adults to depart, leaving players to resolve issues of unequal numbers or unfairly matched teams. With no one watching, they may have achieved what was missing in our contests.

Chapter 35

Year 8–A Player Gains Confidence

DESPITE THE PROBLEMS and mental anguish associated with losing most of our games, Wade's team didn't quit. They signed up for soccer and advanced another year to a larger field and 8v8 format. Our club split the girls off and consolidated them on an all-girls team comprising grades five through eight. Our well-trained girls were solid players, better than some of the boys, and I was sorry to see them go. Occasionally, I saw them when our practices or games coincided.

There was powerlessness associated with being a recreational coach. Players got moved around by the club as needed to fill out rosters. Parents advocated for their players to move on or off a team. I was not consulted when those changes were made. They just flowed downhill and became my responsibility, disclosed on the new roster I received at the coaches' meeting. The girls' reassignment was compensated by adding three new players to the team. One of them, Peter, affirmed that despite our consistent losing record, some parents understood our struggle and were grateful for my efforts.

Peter was well-behaved and athletic—a coach's dream. His dad passed away when he was younger, leaving only him and his mom. He was a year younger than Wade, but the coach for his age group had a reputation for being a negative, angry yeller. Peter's mom was probably hoping for something better by moving him to our team. I didn't know Peter's background when he was assigned to the team. Eventually, Judy learned of it and looped me in, but it didn't matter—I treated everyone the same. What did matter was that Peter was a target of bullying at school because of his stature. He was small for his age, and it affected his confidence. It took me a while to piece together what was going on. But two events hinted at it.

The first happened at practice and was not subtle. It involved another new player, Jack, who was significantly larger and a year older than Peter. In an interaction that lasted only seconds, I watched Jack stalk Peter from behind, bear-hug him, pick him up, and slam him to the ground. Then Jack thrust out his chest, pounded it like an ape, and roared. Peter didn't do anything to provoke the attack—Jack suffered from a lack of verbal and physical self-control.

I reacted immediately. "Jack!" I shouted. "He's your teammate. That's not how you treat your teammate."

At his core, Jack was a good kid; he hung his head and apologized, "Sorry, Mr. Beers."

"Don't apologize to me," I said. "I'm not the one you threw to the ground."

"Sorry, Peter," Jack responded.

His apology sounded sincere but too automatic. Sometimes, words don't matter. Jack's behavior suggested that his loss of control was not unusual. Players on our team respected each other, probably because they had been together for years and suffered together. I accepted Jack's words, but he crossed a line and had to earn redemption with his actions. I sent him on the first and only punishment run that I ever administered. Peter was fine. He brushed the event off and moved on while I mulled it over.

The second hint came after I spent a practice teaching pushing. In general, pushing is not allowed in soccer. However, "fair charging" is a legal form of pushing that occurs when two players contest a ball. Since both players have a right to possess the ball, they can push with their shoulder to move opponents out of the way. I demonstrated the skill with Wade, then told everyone to find a partner. The lesson was messy but fun—boys love an excuse to push. Everyone got a couple of turns, and then we moved on with practice. I wasn't sure if anyone had learned the technique. However, I knew that, at a minimum, I formalized what a few were already attempting.

At the next game, Peter was matched against an opponent who liked to sprint down the sideline with the ball. On several occasions, Peter chased his opponent down until they were abreast and jumped up to match his shoulder against the other player's. Each time he jumped, he fell behind and had to run to catch up. The technique didn't work because he kept losing a step. Peter was lucky not to have been penalized because it looked like he was bashing other players with his body rather than trying to nip in and take the ball. I realized that he had misinterpreted my instructions or that I failed to make them explicit. Peter was trying to put his shoulder on the other player's shoulder so he could push, but it was impossible because he was shorter than his opponent.

When it was Peter's turn to rest, I called him aside and made his weakness his strength, "You have a low center of gravity. Use that to your advantage. Keep your feet on the ground. Don't jump. Just put your shoulder against him and push him off the ball."

Occasionally, I said the right thing at the right time, and a player instantly nailed a task. There was no epiphany in Peter's demeanor. He stood listening to what I said, breathing fast, his cheeks flushed red from exertion.

"Okay," was his only affirmation.

After a quick breather, I sent Peter back onto the field. He was an intelligent and coachable player who didn't jump anymore. Instead, I watched as he began to master the technique, getting stronger and more confident on each occasion.

We took a team picture at the end of that season. Peter posed with his teammates, wedged between William and Ben, two of our best players, while one of our goalkeepers stood behind them, one arm draped around William's neck and the other forearm propped on Peter's shoulder. They all wore smudges of mud on their knees and a look of self-assurance. Jack stood at the other end of the lineup, a little distance from the rest of the team—isolated.

I was often surprised by the positive things that grew out of soccer. When I taught Peter to push, it seemed that act changed his life. I can't take all the credit; his mom advocated for him and got him on a team with older boys. That's the sort of thing that sends a message to bullies. From uncertain and bullied to confident and accomplished, all it took was a soccer tactic. Peter developed the skill to take a soccer ball from Jack anytime he wanted and became one of our most valuable players.

THE GIRLS' DEPARTURE led to changes in team dynamics. Some boys became more uninhibited, and there was a noticeable uptick in belching and farting. The increase coincided with Jack's enlistment; he may have been responsible. One thing was sure, the loss of the girls coincided with a change in staff—Coach Pete went with them, and Coach Charlotte had a conflict with practices. Those circumstances left me without an assistant. The parents didn't seem to care, but Coach Carl, a soccer zealot who had become our club president, was on my back about it. It was frustrating because I had appealed to the parents to get a second adult at practices and games, but no one was willing to take the job. I was also frustrated because although Carl had an assistant, they rarely attended trainings together. The assistant only appeared when Carl couldn't participate in practice.

Requiring a second adult to be present at practices was a general league regulation to ensure the safety of players and coaches. Having a second adult present reduced the potential for improper activity and provided a safety net in case of emergency. Although Coach Carl complied with the requirement on paper, only one coach usually attended his practices. That type of double standard sucked the fun right out of coaching. I tried to comply with the regulations. I sent notes home for three weeks with the team, passing on the message that we needed another coach. The third week was the charm. Jack's dad, Bob, rearranged his work schedule and appeased President Carl.

Chapter 36

No Home Field Advantage

W E WERE AN eleven-boy team playing 8v8 soccer. Victories were scarce, but we scored some goals and were competitive. The near-miss wins were the most frustrating. One game was notable because of how we lost—the referee manipulated the game.

Referee Sam was one of our home-field officials who had a reputation for doing what he could to keep games close. I learned that tidbit from Owen's Coach Henry, who mentioned it one day during practice. If one team jumped out ahead of the other, Sam purportedly made judgments that slowed their attack. He did it by calling offside or pushing. I hadn't met Sam, so I couldn't match his face to his reputation. However, I remembered Henry's words, and when one of our home-field referees imposed his will, I understood what was going on.

I looked forward to the game that day because we played at home against a familiar team. Our games against them were always close, often ending in ties. Historically, they were like us—coed—but that had changed. On that day, we were the all-boys team. Our opponent had one exceptionally tall and lean player who always gave us trouble. He was easy to spot, so when I saw him warming up, we planned our defense. The game began better than I had hoped; no adjustments were necessary. William was smoking hot, and the other team couldn't stop him. He scored three goals in about ten minutes, and we jumped out to an early 3-0 lead. I felt disbelief, relief, and joy that it would be a winning day for our team. I was in the unusual position of being the coach of the dominant club in what looked to be a one-sided game, so I started thinking about what I could do to slow William down.

Referee Sam must have been thinking the same thing. It looked like the same old story to him—a coed team getting beat up by an all-boys team. Referee Sam stepped in. From that moment, whenever William touched the ball, Sam blew his whistle and invented an infraction to award possession of the ball to the other team. After the first whistle, William was unphased and still flying high; he didn't understand what was happening, nor did I. The imaginary infraction occurred midfield, so Sam awarded a free kick to the other team. William backed up and waited for the ball to be put into play. When the kick came, it was weak and misdirected, William anticipated where it would go. He jumped in quickly, cutting it off from the opposing player, and took possession. Sam blew his whistle immediately. William hadn't violated any law of the game and looked confused about what he was doing wrong.

I was starting to suspect that Sam had his thumb on the scale. After the third erroneous whistle, I was sure what was going on. William had been penalized three times in as many minutes, which had never happened before and never happened again. After the fourth whistle, William got the point. Beaten into submission and utterly defeated, he was subdued by the frustrating reality that, for some reason, every time he touched the ball, one of the things that he loved most, the referee took it away from him. It was difficult to watch because I felt like one of my own was being bullied, and I was powerless to stop it.

William's family wasn't wealthy. They didn't have great jobs or a fancy house. They were working stiffs who cared for their kids and lived modestly. As a farm kid with little money, William had a strong work ethic that paid dividends for a few moments at the beginning of our game when he was an unstoppable force, leading his team to a rare victory. But William's parents had also taught him to respect authority; consequently, he was conflicted by the referee's unfair behavior. Ultimately, William did what his parents had ingrained in him and accepted the referee's not-so-subtle message to back off the attack. I could see the disappointment and confusion on William's face as his self-esteem roller coaster bottomed out.

With William's defeat and the referee's help, the game went the other way. I don't know if the tall kid was sitting out, asleep, or hurt at the beginning of the game, but he began to exert his influence. By halftime, the opposing team was ahead by one goal. As players came to the sideline, I directed them to get a drink and was optimistic. I didn't talk about what was transpiring with the referee. Instead, I encouraged the Timberwolves, "We're playing well. We can beat a one-player team because he will get tired. Keep fighting, and the goals will come."

The second half was a battle. We played well defensively and stifled the tall player, but the other team succeeded in scoring again. Two goals down, we kept working, and our opponent seemed to be getting tired. I checked my watch. With ten minutes remaining, I hoped we could still manage a win. I shifted players around on the field to increase our attack. At five minutes, nothing had changed because we couldn't get past their defense. The other coach had made adjustments too. As time elapsed, according to my watch, I accepted that we would lose a game we should have won. Then something happened; time didn't run out.

Sometimes, referees add stoppage time at the end of soccer games, but it wasn't the norm in our league. I was confused but grateful; it felt as if a violation of the space-time continuum had paused the clocks in our little part of the cosmos, allowing us to score another goal, or maybe two. I wondered if Referee Sam had lost track of time or was giving us a chance to tie the game. I kept coaching, hoping for a miracle. At five minutes past the putative end of the match, I wanted to substitute tired players, but it was so close to what I presumed was the end of the game that it wasn't worth trying because referees usually didn't allow it. At ten minutes, I lost hope for victory; there was no sign of the old William, and our players were exhausted. At fifteen minutes, the opposing coach queried Sam about how much time remained, then turned to me and asked what I had for time. I looked at my watch and replied, "My watch shows the game should have ended fifteen minutes ago." The contest continued for three more minutes before Sam whistled an end to it.

After the handshake, I was upbeat, even if the team was dejected, and said, "I'm proud of how we played today. For most of the game, we shut down that tall kid. You mauled him and took him out of the game. It was awesome."

"Yeah, but we lost," Peter responded.

I couldn't hold back; it would have been a lie of omission.

I waved my hand dismissively, "Oh, that was the referee. He manipulated the game. We can't control that." I didn't give details. Then I added, "Forget the score. It was a great game. I'll see you on Tuesday."

I was within earshot of Sam and saw him look up. I didn't intend for him to hear my comments, but I couldn't lie to the team.

It was not the first time I experienced a referee manipulating a game. But it was the first time a referee reversed the lead and absolutely the only time I witnessed what looked and felt like bullying by an official.

I understood what Referee Sam tried to do. He was a volunteer like me, and his heart was in the right place. His goal was to make the game fun and he did what he could to keep the contest close to protect the defeated from embarrassment. If the roles were reversed, I would have appreciated his help, but I would have felt guilty about the victory being stolen.

I wish Sam hadn't heard my comments, but I don't regret what I said or doubt he tampered with the game. I knew we played well enough to win that sunny fall afternoon. It would have been nice if it were official.

Chapter 37

Megan Starts Soccer

THAT FALL, MY coaching duties expanded with Megan's enrollment in U6 soccer. I didn't feel strongly about her participation. It wasn't a dream come true or my worst nightmare, but another turn of the crank in fatherhood. Soccer had infiltrated our family, and she wanted to play. Judy and I couldn't refuse because the game offered the same fitness and character-building opportunities for Megan that it did for her brothers.

Megan always impressed us with her physical ability. The first clue of soccer potential came just before she turned two years old. I carried her into our living room and put her down without noticing the ball in the center of the floor. As her feet touched the ground, she charged out of my hands straight at the ball, kicked it with her stumpy little foot, and then dribbled it across the room using both feet before tee-tering to a stop within a fraction of an inch of the TV. It was frightening and remarkable. There was no way of knowing if she had done it intentionally or accidentally. Judy and I looked at each other in amazement and wondered if what we had witnessed hinted at the future.

There were other suggestions of innate athleticism. Judy

noticed that at junior gymnastics Megan often successfully executed moves on her first try while other girls struggled. In our own home, Megan frequently accomplished physical feats that would have ended in disaster for her brothers. Challenges like using a rough-hewn log or a high wall as a balance beam enticed her. Rock-hopping her way across a creek was easy. Running ahead into closing elevators or busy parking lots was alarmingly common. Judy and I were experienced parents and thought we had seen it all. So, when we saw Megan lining up to do something with a high risk of injury, we tried to stop her.

"Megan, please don't do that. Megan, please don't. Megan, STOP!"

She never listened. She executed the move and walked away with a smug expression as if to say, "See, I told you I could do it." When Owen or Wade attempted the same tasks, scrapes and torn pants were often the outcome.

Megan's first soccer team comprised five girls and four boys. It was an in-house program, so we did not travel to play teams in other communities. Instead, we practiced once a week for less than an hour and scrimmaged ourselves. Building skills and having fun was the name of the game. From my perspective, that was easy. Even better, another dad, Jason, had played soccer in high school and wanted to coach. I volunteered to help him; we made a good team. His coaching philosophy was similar to mine. He liked to get every player involved with a ball, and we dribbled around cones, passed, and played fast-paced mini-games. If he had a competitive streak, it didn't show because we didn't compete against other teams.

THE BEGINNING OF Megan's soccer experience marked the end of my coaching interactions with Owen. Saddled with Wade's team and Megan's practices, it wasn't realistic for me to assist Owen's coaches, so I gave it up. Owen regretted my absence, but my role had been minimal. I chased balls and occasionally pointed out things that needed work. Henry and Felix always seemed grateful for my help, but they didn't need me. Their team struggled with too few players, especially during football season, and wasn't doing well. Owen probably hoped that my involvement would somehow lead to a positive solution. He and I experienced our share of successes over our seven years of soccer together, but I had no magic bullet for the current problems. It was time for my role to end because Megan needed me more.

I felt regret about the transition. Fortunately, my disappointment was softened by a new opportunity. A coach from another team had noticed Owen and inquired if he would like to join them for tournament play. After a quick investigation, we accepted the invitation. It was a valuable opportunity for Owen. His home team was struggling, but the tournaments were fun. Being surrounded by players of higher caliber helped him up his game, and he became a standout defender.

Chapter 38

Vice President Beers

WINTER CAME AND went. Coach Carl, the president of our Soccer Club, asked me to act as vice president, and I agreed. I didn't want the job, but in a small town, many volunteer positions were filled by the same few individuals. I thought I couldn't refuse. The post was vacant and had to be filled for official purposes. When Carl asked me to take the job, he didn't mention an additional responsibility, but I suspected he secretly wanted me to fill the president-elect position—intending that, ultimately, I would be promoted to president. He didn't ask, so I didn't object, but there was no way I was taking that job.

Chapter 39

Jungle Run

MY CHALLENGE FOR the spring season was to make the experience fun and new for Wade's team. We still had players who struggled with fundamentals, so it was hard to abandon basic drills. I needed something novel to keep players engaged. With the girls' departure, the team acted like a bunch of guys interested in guy things. Military themes and sports were popular topics. I rolled with those tendencies and introduced the Jungle Run.

After a long winter, nearly all our players needed some endurance work, and the soccer fields were wet in early spring, so it seemed like a great time to do some running. It was my attempt to make fitness fun while playing to the urge to be part of a team—the animal side that wants to run like a wolf pack. When I introduced the idea, the team was enthusiastic, but I was apprehensive about losing someone. The run wasn't easy. Players who lacked endurance might stop, and we had a few naturalists who could be easily distracted by a frog or a butterfly. I made them all swear to return.

"All right, you all have to promise to come back," I said as I looked at them. "Hold up your right hand and repeat after me."

I held up my hand and adopted a posture suitable for administering an oath. The boys followed my example.

"I solemnly swear to stick together and return to the soccer field because I love soccer."

The boys mumbled their responses in jumbled unison.

"Now spit," I said, turning my head and directing a dry *ptooey* toward the ground.

Again, the crew followed my example and affirmed their conviction with action, some with more flare than others. That done, I turned and led the way.

When I conceived the Jungle Run, I explored a snowmobile trail adjacent to our practice field. The run was approximately one mile. It ascended a long hill from the soccer field for the first quarter, then turned left into woods, dodging stumps, over logs, and winding around shrubs. It wasn't easy because the ground was covered with leaves, wet, and boggy. I worried that someone would twist an ankle. The path broke out of the woods for a short distance, then another left turn, and back down the hill to the soccer field.

Apart from the ankle twists, I had two main concerns. The first was that if it rained, the trail could get muddy, really muddy, suck-the-shoes-right-off-your-feet muddy. I didn't want to start practice poking around looking for some kid's $120 pair of shoes. My second concern was I thought I recognized stinging nettles at the edge of the woods. The scientific name for the stinging nettle, *Urtica*, stems from a Latin root meaning "I burn." The stems and leaves of the shrub are covered with spines that, like tiny hypodermic needles, inject a cocktail of acids and irritants into the skin of anything that brushes against them. The lightest touch results in an itchy, burning sensation and a mild rash. When I scouted the trail, the nettles were only about six inches tall and difficult to identify. A week later, when we made the inaugural run, they had grown to about two feet tall—exactly the right height to assault soccer players' uncovered thighs, hands, and arms.

As I ran toward the woods that day, I was sure of my identification when I saw the more mature plants, but there was no stopping. The wolf pack would have ripped me to shreds. So, I shouted, "Watch the nettles," and pointed as I plunged ahead without losing a step. The gauntlet was short; it only fringed the woods. Once we broke through, the trail was clear, and the rest of the run went as planned. When we reassembled at the field, I quickly checked for acute reactions. Everyone was a little out of breath but alright, so our invigorated—if slightly burned—group pushed on through a productive practice.

The Jungle Run was a hit. At the next practice, the team wanted to go again. I argued against it because the nettles grew larger and more abundant each day. Players implored me, led by an impassioned Jack who was not built to run, yet he begged to go up that hill. I let them go but warned, "I'll time you. You all have to beat my time." While they ran, I set up practice, then called out elapsed times when they returned. They were as good as their word.

The goal of the Jungle Run was to build on the previous season's successes by improving our endurance, but the reward was the same—we lost our first game. The week after the loss, I felt dejected as I walked from the parking lot to the practice field with the ball bag in one hand and the gear bag in the other. Coaching Wade's team had become the most challenging thing I had ever done. Always trying to emulate a positive attitude while feeling like I had let the team down was getting old. The gear bags had never seemed so heavy. Part of me wanted to quit, walk away, and move on; part of me felt bound by a commitment to the team. One path was easy, and the other felt soul-crushing.

The only courses of action I could think of were to pray or look for an indication that what I was doing was good. I didn't pray.

As I walked, I was joined by several players. They hovered around, putting on sweatshirts or conversing. The fabric handle of the gear bag cut into my hand, so I stopped and emptied both hands to readjust. My back hurt. I paused, trying to loosen it up, when I noticed William. He was awkwardly straddling the ball bag, toggling back and forth, first on one foot, then the other, like a dog anxiously trying to figure out how to retrieve a favorite toy out of reach. The bag was knotted shut, and he struggled because he didn't know how to open it. Finally, he asked me, "Can I get a ball?" I opened the bag, and the hovering players all grabbed a ball and ran ahead. *That was the sign*, I thought. All they wanted to do was play.

PLAYING GOT ME through the week. Then we lost another game. The only thing to do for that was ice cream. Wade and I routinely stopped for ice cream on the drive home after a game. It helped alleviate the pain of embarrassing defeats— as if the cure for a bruised ego was to rub ice cream on it. Many soccer fields were on the edge of towns. Often, there were few choices, but it seemed essential to obtain the psychological salve as quickly as possible, so we sought out the first quick mart that could supply what we needed no matter how sketchy the establishment looked. After a few trips, we developed a short list of favorite spots. It gave us something to look forward to after taking a sound thumping.

We sat on a curb or picnic table and ate silently while the sugar and ice-creamy goodness flowed through our veins. Those occasions were a time of bonding when Wade and I consumed our frozen delicacies separately but together. It was a way to put the past behind us and revive our self-respect as our frustration melted away like the bars we ate. As good as it was, it was even better when we won a game.

Chapter 40

Divided Purples

IT WAS MENTALLY difficult for me to prepare the team to play the Purples. Our players knew from experience what the game would be like—and that there was no escape. We never had an attendance problem when we faced the Purples. That *esprit de corps* deserved the truth from me, so when I spoke before the game, I emphasized doing the work, striving for personal bests, and having fun by playing together. Then I mustered more enthusiasm and a quicker pace as I prepared the team for the field.

"Be ready to play at the whistle; don't let them catch you sleeping," I said. "Pass well to keep possession because if we have the ball, they don't. Fight the ball off to the side, then up the line. Keep working and raise your hand if you are hurt or tired."

It was a good speech, and I meant it. Playing our game was the only way to survive the day with our self-respect intact—unless something changed.

On that day, it did.

During warm-up, I noticed that the Purples' usual coach was absent. I attributed it to a substitution for the day because the club was the same, and I recognized the uniforms and some players. In fact, it wasn't the Purples. It was a team composed of players who were either passed over or had declined to join the Purples—the Reciprocal Purples. When we warmed up, I did not know what was in store. I had no idea that the Reciprocals existed. Had I known, I probably would have asked our league to schedule us against them instead of their super-competitive counterpart.

The contest against the Reciprocals demonstrated the disservice to the community created by establishing the Purples' select team. There was no parity; it wasn't fair. Our team played what we practiced, and the goals racked up. By the end of the first half, frustrated parents were on the sideline berating the Reciprocals' coach, yelling at her to do something. It wasn't the coach's fault that their soccer community was divided. The Purples' coach was ahead of everyone else in skill, knowledge, and organization. He had skimmed off all the best players for his select team and left the rest of the community to deal with the aftermath. It was an unexpectedly good day for the Timberwolves because we thought we would suffer a ruthless pounding; instead, we played our game and defeated an average team that wasn't much different from ours. It was a welcome reward for facing a challenge.

Chapter 41

Owen's Evolution

T HAT SPRING, I watched Owen pass through another threshold I never saw coming. He was in eighth grade, participating in his last rec soccer season. His team fared slightly better in the spring because it wasn't competing with tackle football for players. Combining U13 and U14 age groups gave them enough players to field a team. The combined team had weaknesses and relied heavily on a few older boys.

As I watched the two teams warm up, I couldn't help but notice one player on the other team. He was dark-skinned, a little taller than Owen, and muscular. He didn't look like a typical thirteen-year-old soccer player; he looked like a sixteen-year-old football player. He was conspicuous because he had a giant mop of curly black hair, which he controlled with a headband so that it necked down at the top of his head and then blossomed above. I could tell he was a skilled player from how he moved through the warm-up drills with a confident spring in his step. I was worried about what was going to happen. I had seen it too many times—a player like that could slice through a combination team filled with young players like ours, and that's how the game started.

His team passed him the ball, and he did the rest. He ran past our inexperienced players, who were either afraid or too unskilled to stop him. Someone nearby in the stands joked that his birth certificate was probably lost, implying that he was undocumented and in the wrong age group. It was a slur. I doubt it would have been used if his skin and hair were lighter, but I understood their frustration because he was much better and physically stronger than all the other players. It could have been that, like the Giants, he had been held back at an early age and allowed to stay with his cohort even though he was older. He could also have excelled because he played more soccer than our players. He ran all over the field, right through almost everyone, until Owen's coach adjusted. He told Owen to mark him, to stay on him no matter what, and stop him. He probably used some idiom like "Stick to him like glue." Whatever he told him, it worked. Owen shut him down. Either his teammates didn't pass to him because he was covered, or if he did receive the ball, he couldn't escape with it. It was amazing to watch, like a perpetual one-on-one drill.

The skilled player pushed hard with his shoulder, and Owen gave as good as he got. One of the parents took pictures with a telephoto lens that day, and they caught some of the action. The photos show two players, laser-focused on the ball, shoulders together, each leaning into the other so that their bodies made the shape of an inverted V. The confrontation was aggressive but fair. It ended at the half when the opposing team's coach moved the kid to goalkeeper. Without him on the field, the two sides were evenly matched. The game was a loss for our team but an amazing, eye-opening day for me. I had never seen Owen play like that. It wasn't boys rec soccer played for fun; it was a battle between two men.

After the game, Owen was quiet. I don't think he enjoyed it because the spotlight was not his thing. He would have preferred the game to be more of a joint effort, but his teammates were too fractured and unskilled to help. It was a personal victory for Owen, and a proud day for me, tinged with regret because my little soccer buddy was growing up.

AS OWEN'S SEASON wrapped up, I took up a collection for an end-of-season thank-you gift for his coaches—no one else was doing anything for them. I was emboldened because I wasn't assisting the team anymore, so at the second-to-the-last game, I made the rounds. I sought out all the parents I could find and asked for donations. I was grateful to a few folks who lined up to contribute. Their actions affirmed that I was not alone in my opinion that Henry and Felix deserved acknowledgment for their efforts. Unfortunately, most parents made me hunt them down, even though I think they knew what I was doing. Hunting was difficult because some parents watched the game from their cars in the parking lot. I hunted the crowd in the bleachers, then the fans seated along the sideline. As I walked back to sit down, I spotted what I knew to be a wealthy parent in a car. As I approached, they noticed me, panicked, and urgently fumbled for their phone. It wasn't ringing—it was an excuse not to give me $5 or $10 (there were two coaches) for a gift. For several awkward, embarrassing moments, I lingered at the driver's door, watching the fumbling, waiting for the occupant to stop the act and roll down the window so I could ask the obvious question. Finally, they did but wouldn't part with a penny. They promised to get it to me at the next practice but never did.

At the ceremony after Owen's last game, I gave a speech and expressed my gratitude to Henry and Felix. I summarized their commitment and the hours invested each season: seven Saturdays or Sundays devoted to games; two practices, and a game, plus preparation worked out to about seven hours per week, assuming zero drive time, plus two weeks of training before the first game totaled about fifty-five hours each season; transporting players who didn't have rides; attending coaching clinics and Soccer Club meetings; doing the job in any weather; all multiplied by eight years. We owed them a debt of gratitude. They got a round of applause, a six-pack, a gift certificate, and a hearty handshake from me and a few others.

WADE'S TEAM ENDED the season with two wins and several near misses. There was a consensus that we should do something to celebrate the end of another soccer cycle together. Trophies were definitely out of the question. I suggested team T-shirts and the parents agreed. I surfed the internet and found the profile of a howling wolf, and I arranged each player's name in a circle around it. Judy had the image printed onto T-shirts, and we handed them out after our last game, which was at home. We ate pizza and cake, and the team awarded me a sports-themed ceramic plate signed by all the players.

I had made it through another year! Wade seemed to

enjoy our time together, Owen received invitations to play tournaments, and Megan's team had a successful in-house season. Happy soccer players all around. Only eight more years to go.

Chapter 42

Letters of Commendation

A WEEK LATER, I wrote my first letter commending a player. I wrote it because expressing admiration for another person can help them overcome imposing challenges, but only if it is received at the appropriate time.

Encouraging a player is a tricky undertaking. Too much encouragement from a coach can produce jealousy in teammates who crave attention; too little, and the feat of excellence demonstrated by a player escapes recognition as it melts into the background of everyday activities. Some aspects of William's behavior deserved to be recognized. I did not want to let the opportunity slip away because experience had taught me that the timing of a compliment is as vital as the words offered.

When I worked at the university, I was a self-funded research scientist. I toiled for years, trying to do what I thought were the right things to be successful. The problem was that the lifestyle was inconsistent with a successful marriage, and enough divorced colleagues surrounded me to prove it. Eventually, Judy and I concluded that a move back to our home state was best and began announcing our intentions. In the following weeks, we experienced a series of admiration-filled interactions. In one instance, a woman we did not know introduced herself to Judy and thanked her for what she had done for the school and community. She had a child in the same school as our boys and was aware of a litany of things Judy and I did, including coaching soccer. She thanked Judy for all of it. I also heard from colleagues who surprised me with how they perceived the scope and value of my accomplishments.

Before we announced our departure, Judy and I had no idea that anyone was aware of our activities. Some conversations even went so far as to encourage us to stay and made us feel a little guilty for leaving, although I doubted that guilt was the intended purpose. It felt great to be appreciated, but the admiration didn't change anything because it came too late. A chain of events was already underway, and we were leaving town. Had we known our activities were so valued, we might have found a way to continue. We could have evaluated other possibilities, like changing jobs or careers without relocating. Making decisions like that would have involved weighing alternatives, and the process would not have been easy. A few words of encouragement might have changed our assessment.

I wanted William to make thoughtful decisions. I knew he was competitive and probably took our losses to heart. He was also struggling in school, and his parents were using soccer as an incentive to get him to study. I decided that the best thing was to write him a letter of encouragement, telling him that he was doing the right thing and that I knew how hard he was working:

William,

I am writing to express my appreciation for your efforts on the soccer field. Every week, I appoint different players to act as team captains. I rotate captains so everyone can experience what it is like, but I want you to know that because of your actions, you are our real Team Captain. Practice after practice, and year after year, you lead the team. Your teammates follow you because you have great athletic ability, work hard, and play fair. They also follow you because you treat them with respect and as equals, even if they are not as good at soccer as you.

You are a natural leader, but you cannot lead when you miss practice due to incomplete schoolwork. Your education is essential for your future and schoolwork must come before soccer. It does not matter if you are playing in grade school, high school, or college; athletes must always have passing grades before they can compete. So, no matter how hard it seems, get your homework done because it takes more than a strong body to play soccer well—it also takes a strong mind.

I am proud to be your coach. Enjoy your summer. I'll see you on the field this fall.

Coach Andy Beers

My letter accomplished what I had hoped. It gave William confidence and motivated a change in his attitude about homework. He proudly shared his improved scores with me. His dad also thanked me with a firm handshake and a man-to-man moment where his smile expressed gratitude for my encouragement of his son.

I wrote Ben a commendation letter too. He was an incredibly quiet kid, the type who gets overlooked because people forget he is there. He rarely talked to me, always behaved, and did his job. He was our MVP, and that is what I told him. Ben did not break character—he never said a word about my letter. But I knew that at least he was aware that other people noticed his hard work, even if they didn't acknowledge it. Doing the right thing is the right thing to do, and it needs to be encouraged occasionally.

Andy's Advice ... for Experienced Coaches and Parents

Recognize that coaches and players must learn a new system every time teams advance to a larger field. Continue skill development at practices while adding content that fosters teamwork and a big-picture game perspective. Pass, pass, pass.

For coaches:

1. **View every event as an opportunity to learn.** Don't let your competitive nature cloud your judgment or blind you to learning something new from an opposing coach.
2. **Plan so your team succeeds.** Arrange players so weak teammates have support; anticipate unannounced absences on game day; delegate tasks to assistants and parents so you can focus on what is important.
3. **Practice in any weather because you will play in it.** Teach the team to succeed in any conditions.
4. **Emphasize that successful plays come from teamwork.** Acknowledge the contributions of supporting players.
5. **Break up the routine.** Changing the format of practices can spark renewed interest.

For parents:

1. **Don't expect a starring role** if you are an assistant coach. Pitch in to help where needed, which might mean that one day you are a human cone, and the next you are the coach on game day.
2. **Injuries happen; don't panic.** Help if you can because most coaches are not medical professionals. Have a plan in place if your player is injured.
3. **Forcing a child to play** because you contend that "It will be good for them" can lead to discord on the team. Some players may grow to love the sport, but others will be defiant. Parents of unmotivated players

should evaluate their child's performance and attitude. Work with the coach to find a solution that works for all.

4. **Remind your player that their school performance matters.** Soccer players must maintain passing grades to compete in high school and beyond.

5. **Don't stop playing in the off-season.** Encourage your player to participate in a soccer camp during the off-season. Inquire about the availability of scholarships if the cost is prohibitively high.

Chapter 43

Year 9–Losers' Walk

THE FALL SEASON brought changes for Owen. He started high school and joined the soccer team. Most players on the squad were familiar to him, either from his hometown or the tournament team. He liked the coach, who had military experience and used mind games to make tough workouts fun. If his coach observed a player standing with arms crossed, the punishment was that the entire team ran a mile.

The message was twofold. First, if players were comfortable enough to cross their arms, they needed to work harder. It was simple mechanics of human ambulation—arms swing in unison with moving feet. Second, individual actions affect the unit. If one player lapsed and thoughtlessly crossed their arms out of habit, the entire team endured the exercise. The team ran as a consequence of the actions of one of their own. Pain and sweat were the shared currency; peer pressure and the knowledge that others suffered due to individual actions were the commodities of the transaction. On the few occasions when there were no infractions, Owen's coach purposely crossed his arms, and the team ran with the knowledge that they had succeeded and were awarded the workout because it was good for them.

Owen's team was competitive, and he enjoyed it. He made varsity as a freshman but didn't see much playing time because they had a full roster and few injuries. We chalked it up to experience and assumed that his turn would come in years ahead.

COACH JASON AND I did a repeat for Megan's team, another year of in-house play. We expanded existing skills and kept the workouts fun. We increased the frequency of practices to two days each week because the team seemed ready for it. They were more aggressive and competent than Wade's group had been at the same age—especially Jason's son, who had benefited from playing soccer with his dad and older brothers. He was small for his age and looked like a happy little soccer elf with red curly hair and freckles. With the charismatic glow of a successful leader, he was aggressive but well-behaved, with no attitude. His skill and decorum were valuable because he modeled good behavior for the rest of the team, making them better by challenging and demonstrating what was possible. Coach Jason and I didn't miss the competitiveness of playing official games that season, but we thought the team was ready for the next step. They were above average in skill, and there were no butterfly catchers; everyone seemed focused on playing soccer. We had won the soccer-team lottery, and we knew it.

WADE'S TEAM REMAINED a challenge. I suspected it was our last chance to win games because when we advanced to the 11v11 division the following year, we would suffer the same low-numbers problem Owen's team encountered. I tried to keep our practices fresh by introducing new drills and fun games with great names like Power and Finesse and World Cup Soccer. Our practices were well attended and fun, but the work didn't translate into wins for various reasons. Our biggest weakness was that the team included players from several age groups. The physical immaturity and lack of experience of our younger players left us vulnerable to more seasoned squads. Our performance against the Reciprocals showed that we could successfully compete with average teams. Still, we lacked the critical mass to win against teams we played regularly.

I took our win/loss record to heart because there were additional things that I could have done to make the team better. If I had been more competitive and used B-team filtering to drive off weak players, then scoured other lineups and encouraged capable players to forsake their original squads for my crew, we could have been stronger. I also could have urged players to participate in other programs during the off-season—summer and winter indoor leagues. I didn't do that because I didn't want to be responsible for managing another team. Lastly, I worked five days a week from 6:30 a.m. to 4 p.m., had a spouse, three children, a house, and two cars. I was unwilling to invest more time into soccer because our family had other important things to do. There was more to life than soccer, even if it meant our team would suffer a losing record.

Consequently, things stayed the same for the Timberwolves during the last two seasons of 8v8 soccer. We were lucky to eke out a win each season. I got through it by telling myself to keep a long-term view, that I was training players so that they could excel in high school. That approach had worked for Owen. If we kept improving, the boys on the team would at least have the skills to succeed in the future.

One frustrating trend was that our games ended more frequently in lopsided shutouts. It was embarrassing and disheartening to lose by a large margin and be prevented from scoring even a single goal.

When I played high school sports, it was common for teams with a commanding lead to substitute players so less experienced individuals could participate. The custom balanced player skill levels on the field, slowed the pace of scoring without affecting game outcomes, and had its roots in sportsmanship. Much had changed during the years between when I played high school athletics and when I coached rec soccer for my children, but not the philosophy behind good sportsmanship. Still, the Timberwolves routinely played a few teams that attained a large lead, then continued playing aggressively while their B-team players sat on the bench. That type of competitive behavior had a place in some circumstances, like tournaments, but it seemed inappropriate in routine recreational soccer. A team's behavior depended on its coach, some of whom were unyieldingly supercompetitive. Even something intended to promote sportsmanship, like the handshake at the end of a game, could be corrupted by too much competition. There was a name for it: the Losers' Walk.

Losers' Walk was part of the familiar handshake ritual that took place immediately following a game. Without prompting, coaches directed players to form opposing lines at the center of the field. Then the two ranks walked forward to shake hands or high-five each opponent as they passed. The refs stood at midfield and observed as the two teams interacted. Traditionally, this practice made sense because clubs occupied different sides of the field. However, the convention in our league was to have both teams assembled on the same sideline during games. That decision was probably made to aid referees so players from both teams could check in to games from the same location. The solution may have been great for the refs but created another problem because the handshake convention remained the same.

After a game, the losing team was expected to walk the greater distance to the far side of the center of the field so the handshake could occur. The expectation was mostly unspoken. Occasionally, some kid on the winning team would announce, "Losers' Walk," in an annoying sing-song fashion. Other times, if the losing team didn't take the far side, there was an awkward traffic jam as two teams tried to line up on the near side until one of the coaches stepped in. It was demeaning and humiliating to do the Walk as if we were taking part in some medieval tradition where the defeated team was forced to parade in front of a crowd and take punishment. So many idioms exist for how it felt: twist of the knife, rub salt in the wound, in your face. I wondered how the soccer zealots failed to recognize that the custom was inconsistent with the general philosophy of sportsmanship in the league.

I was frustrated because the remedy was obvious. Both teams were already on the same sideline; all they had to do was assemble into opposing lines and walk toward each other to shake hands after a game. That would have alleviated the Losers' Walk and made a sporting end to the competition. No referee or club ever addressed the issue. It might have been a breach of protocol, but I tried to be part of the solution. When the time came for the handshake, I communicated with opposing coaches to meet on the sideline. Most coaches complied, but a few were unaware or unwilling, and we had to follow them out onto the field and do the Walk. When we won a game, I made certain that our opponent knew my offer to conduct the handshake on the sideline. We abandoned the referees in the center of the field, lined up where we stood, and met at the centerline. Our opponent always seemed grateful.

Chapter 44

Bad Things Come in Threes

IN JUNE, I got the phone call I hoped to avoid—Coach Carl, our club president, told me he was stepping down and I was being promoted. For a moment, those famous words, "I shall not seek, and I will not accept, the nomination," rolled through my brain, but I shook off the temptation to echo LBJ and managed a less eloquent, "No, I'm not interested."

"You can't," replied Carl. "It's a rule; that's how it's done."

It was a ridiculous assertion. He was the same guy who encouraged me to have a B team, badgered me about an assistant coach when his second never attended practice, and became president of the club without serving as vice president. He was a soccer zealot who was all about the rules if they didn't apply to him. I stood firm. I was already coaching two soccer teams, felt overworked with my real job, and didn't want the added duties of the president.

"Try to do too much, and you don't do anything well," I said.

I don't know if he took it as a jab, which it wasn't, or if he lacked a rebuttal. He ended the call by hanging up on me.

That was my last official conversation as an officer of the Soccer Board. I dodged that bullet, but not the next one.

A few days later, I received a call from William's dad, who told me that a select team had inquired if William was interested in playing for them. He said William felt terrible about leaving but that it was a good opportunity. I agreed and told him it was fine. I had anticipated the outcome and was surprised it hadn't happened sooner. William lived in the hinterlands, in the country between two towns, with no neighborhood, at the edge of the school district. It wasn't unusual for him to go to school in one place and play sports in another. He came from a hard-working family that didn't have many advantages. They probably thought that athletics was his best path to college—his only path. How could I object? I thanked his dad for calling, hung up the phone, and wrote William another letter wishing him good luck in the future.

Later that summer, Coach Jason knocked at my front door. He was there to pick up another of his sons who was Wade's friend. Judy joined us as we chatted on the front porch, waiting for the boys to wrap things up. We discussed the usual things: the pace of summer, vacations, and the weather. Then, as the boys tumbled down the stairs and bolted out the door, I said something like, "I guess I'll see you in a couple of weeks at the coaches' meeting."

Jason didn't say a word, got wide-eyed, and shifted his weight uncomfortably from one foot to the other.

I continued, trying to fill the awkward silence, "Then we will get things going."

Still silent, Jason avoided eye contact and followed his son to the car.

Judy and I looked at each other as they pulled out of the

driveway. "That was weird," she said as we laughed about the awkward interaction. We were both naive and unsuspecting.

Two weeks later, I drove to the coaches' meeting by myself. I dreaded the meetings because they always seemed to squander a beautiful summer evening. When I worked at the university, a colleague often lamented that organizational meeting participants should be required to stand to motivate them to get through material quickly. My experience confirmed the merit of his observation—lack of urgency in soccer meetings often made them unnecessarily long. There was nothing I could say. I had refused my chance to be president and run things, so when I arrived at the meeting, I located the folding chair with the coach packet marked Timberwolves and sat down. Jason wasn't there, which wasn't unusual. There were several chairs with packets but no coach.

I perused my packet as the meeting started. Wade's team comprised thirteen players from the fifth, sixth, and seventh grades, with nine returning players. That number of players for a fall soccer team in our program wasn't bad. However, the team was composed of individuals of varying ages, so we were in for a rough time. As I broke down the possibilities for the team in my head, I heard my name. Someone from the Soccer Board abruptly handed me what I thought was Jason's packet and said, "You're in charge."

I was confused because no one had inquired if I wanted to coach the team. I assumed they meant, "Pass this material on to Jason," but I was wrong—they meant what they said. Jason had decided to take his son and two of four other boys on the team and join an elite league in a nearby town where he would be their coach. No one at the meeting knew more than that; if they did, they weren't talking. The Soccer Board was oddly closemouthed. I wondered if my trophy history or refusal to act as club president was the cause.

Although I declined the promotion to president because I lacked time to do the job well, I readily accepted the offer to become head coach of Megan's team. Those decisions didn't make sense from a time management standpoint. But I knew that finding someone to act as president would be easier than finding a coach I trusted for Megan's team, so I leaned into my new role and went home with two coach packages, balls, gear bags, and a good story to tell Judy.

Chapter 45

Year 10–Wade's Team Dwindles

THAT FALL, WADE'S team transitioned smoothly to the big field and full-on 11v11 soccer. With nine returning players and Coach Bob as my assistant, we indoctrinated four new teammates. Our skill sets ranged from first-time players to accomplished. The new players brought hybrid vigor to the team but fractured our sense of unity. Some of them, especially the younger players, didn't have the skills or commitment to keep up with the rest. It was a disruption, and it dragged us down. I had seen it before with Owen's team. Our team had more players than his, but inexperience was a problem, especially when I factored in the hormone effect of pitting ten-year-olds against twelve-year-olds. There was nothing I could do about that, so I settled for trying to make practices fun. I must have succeeded because it definitely wasn't the one-sided, scoreless games that kept players on the team.

Our daily agenda was the same as it had always been: warm up, stretch, discuss the plan for the day, review a skill, progress the skill, and play a fun mini-game or scrimmage. Occasionally, I threw the ritual away, the boys cast off their shirts, and we just played a variety of mini-games.

Warm, rainy days were unique because the team loved

to play in the rain and often refused to go home. I regulated the soggy scrimmages as parents waited in the parking lot, ignored, while their boys played on. I let them play because fun practices were the best thing we had going. Thirteen players divided into two teams on a full-size field meant much running was involved. I took the goalkeeper spot for one side to keep players participating. The protocol provided enough organization to keep the game fair and the freedom to play with flexibility. Players pushed themselves out of their usual envelopes, taking shots or running until they were gassed, then walking off their fatigue while someone else had a turn. Laughter and harmless trash talk were ubiquitous.

Those drizzly days were prized because no sun blinded our eyes, and the water-soaked field softened, so cleats found purchase. If a player fell, wet soil gave way against knees and elbows. Humid air prevented mouths from getting dry, and raindrops created white noise, drowning out the rest of the world. All that remained was the squish of wet earth, the smell of grass, and the sound of a teammate calling for the ball. Soccer bliss.

Chapter 46

Marcus's Day

AMID THE MANY losses that fall, there was a moment of individual player growth at an event called the Friendly Tournament. The origin of the Friendly preceded my participation in the soccer program, so I didn't know its background or justification. It was unofficial. Nothing was written down or explained; I didn't even know about it until a week before the tournament when I got a call from our club president telling me that we were supposed to attend and that he had forgotten to tell me sooner. Our official game schedule for the day showed we had a bye—no game. After the phone call, I knew why. The event was a day where all the league's seventh- and eighth-grade teams played each other at one location. It had a fun tournament atmosphere with teams sporting brightly colored soccer uniforms, a concession stand, and hundreds of children chasing soccer balls around the complex of fields. However, there was no trophy, and nothing was friendly about it. In that environment, it was inevitable that there were teams who were in it to win it all. Weak teams that got in their way were cannon fodder. We were scheduled to play three abbreviated games; I hoped that they were teams with which we were closely matched.

The weather was clear and dry, but the temperature was in the nineties—hot for September. Our first game was in the morning. We played well but narrowly missed a win. Despite the loss, I was relieved because I had been nervous about player attendance. Getting players to games was tough in our rural league, where we routinely drove forty miles one-way to play. To coach a successful team, I had to teach players the ins and outs of soccer and train their parents to find remote soccer fields at obscure locations, plan for navigating old towns wrapped around river courses that were once main arteries of commerce, and arrive a half hour before kickoff. Not all parents took those concerns seriously, especially when I gave short notice that it would be an all-day event. Those things created anxiety for me on game day because it didn't matter how hard I worked at practice, if a parent didn't plan to get their player to the event on time, my game plan was disrupted.

On Friendly Day, I was fortunate everyone arrived on time, but after the first game, as the sun rose higher, I could see that some players were not prepared for the heat. Fortunately, we had ninety minutes before our second game, so I located shade for the team and recruited willing parents to solve our hydration problem.

Twenty minutes later, fortified with a cooler filled with ice and beverages, I began preparing for our second game of the day, which was sure to be tough. I didn't expect a win, but I thought we could be competitive if we played well. We stretched and loosened up as game time approached, then took the field. Marcus was our goalkeeper. He was tall, thoughtful, and committed to the team. I liked him and had confidence that he would do his best. However, his best was not enough on that day—Marcus and the team were flat. I didn't know if it was the heat or a lack of preparation for multiple games; whatever the cause, Marcus didn't get support from his teammates, and some easy goals were scored.

I desperately tried to figure out what to do while the shots kept coming, each highlighting Marcus's play. It looked like he was asleep in the goal because he wasn't attacking and missed what I thought were opportunities. He seemed to be having a bad day, and I felt the need to act because we were playing in a "tournament." So, I behaved according to what I thought was expected—I substituted the goalkeeper. I had never done it before, and Marcus took it hard. He came off the field angry and frustrated, throwing his keeper equipment at the gear bag. I knew there was no point in talking until after a cooling-off period. I felt bad because I knew he wanted to play the position, but as a coach, I also sensed an obligation to adjust if someone wasn't playing well.

After a few minutes, Marcus returned to our sideline composed. I talked to him briefly, then sent him back onto the field as a defender and watched an amazing transformation. I don't know if it was anger or adrenaline, but he was not flat anymore. He played like a man possessed, flying around the field, attacking, slicing between opponents and the ball, poking it out, or taking possession. His defensive play was the spark I had been trying to find, and the team began to play more competitively. His behavior was not enough to change the game's outcome, but Marcus played soccer at a higher level from that day forward. He discovered something that hot afternoon when he threw logic and caution away and played with reckless abandon. The path was painful, but he came through the experience a better soccer player because he did not quit.

Marcus's day was fantastic for me as a coach, but I never shared my perspective with him because I feared he remembered it as a failure. For years, it bothered me that I never shared my thoughts even though we were friends. Then, on his eighteenth birthday, the opportunity came. Judy and I were invited to a dinner party in his honor. My gift was a letter recounting my impression of the day. I ended the letter with, "You succeeded because you did not quit. It seems to me that there is a life lesson in that experience. When you face tough challenges, things will not always be as expected. You may have to change tactics or set a new goal, but nothing will change unless you keep doing the work."

I still take that advice to heart when I regret how badly I felt for pulling him from the goal—if I hadn't acted, his personal-growth event would never have occurred, and that wisdom would never have been conveyed.

Chapter 47

Need for Change

THERE WAS A danger in being stoic—complacency. A stoic player or coach doesn't scream or jump up and down but is as much or more involved in the game as one who does. Stoics put their maximum effort on the field so that they uphold their responsibility to the team. In contrast, complacent players attend practices and games but lack determination and go through the motions without trying to improve. Unfortunately, I thought I was starting to see complacency creep into the Timberwolves, especially in some younger players.

Another danger was the risk of becoming entombed in stoicism. Entombed players and coaches trudge on, working, trying to do better, and failing to respond when change is needed. I was afraid the team was starting to trudge. I worried a pattern was developing where players attended practice out of obligation to me and I to them. We were doggedly marching forward together when we should have executed a Plan B.

The Plan B that I contemplated was dissolving the team and joining another local club. Our school district was small, and our high school did not offer soccer. It had barely enough bodies to assemble a football team, so it partnered with another district to meet the needs of those who wanted to play soccer. The solution made sense because both schools struggled independently, but together, they had enough players for a varsity and sometimes a junior varsity. I reasoned that players from the two schools would ultimately be combined when they reached high school, so why not make a move now? Merging allowed our players of various ages to be reassigned into appropriate divisions. The trouble was that dissolving our team and leaving our soccer club without seventh- or eighth-grade squads was anathema to many soccer zealots. The proposition flew in the face of civic pride. Those capstone eleven-player teams were hallmarks of successful programs. Convincing people to give that up wouldn't be easy. Their desire for a thriving organization closed their eyes to our struggle, but denial didn't solve our problems.

Chapter 48

Trip to the Emergency Room

MEGAN'S TEAM WAS a different story—one of hope for a new beginning. The loss of Coach Jason and the three skilled boys he lured away, combined with the addition of four new players, made me feel like I was starting over from scratch with the team. In addition, we transitioned to competitive 4v4 games. I convened a team meeting to explain the implications of those changes to parents. No longer would we leisurely assemble at our home field for fun and games. Going forward, there would be maps to help families navigate to far-off games, a snack and drink schedule, uniform and shoe requirements, and the need for someone to volunteer as an assistant coach. The parents had a few questions. Everything sorted itself out once I dispelled the confusion about what happened to Coach Jason. One parent, Paul, volunteered to be my assistant. He was a first-time coach and a little unsure, but he played soccer in high school, and my first impression was good; I thought we would get along well. With that foundation, Paul and I began training our new team.

The scope of skill levels was broad and ranged from exceptional to toddler-like. One boy, Jacob, seemed too young for the team. It was as if he operated on a different plane of awareness—the cosmic void where life forms wore blank stares and were prone to drifting through space without intention. He had never played before and was strangely clingy. He liked me, often wanting to hold my hand and stay at my side during practices and games. I didn't know how to handle his behavior because my hands were usually full, and eleven other players needed my attention. Consequently, Jacob didn't get much coddling. I dispensed a version of tough love that was patient, positive, and firm. I encouraged him to get involved in activities while avoiding his gaze as he stared up at me with affectionate puppy-dog eyes. Then I peeled his sticky, sweaty hand from mine and half pushed, half towed him onto the field. Jacob complied grudgingly but without tears. I suspected he was accustomed to being treated that way by his teachers and other adults to whom he became attached because maybe he needed a dad.

Another boy, Emil, communicated by meowing, which surprised me when his parents introduced us. I started the conversation with a handshake, "Hi, Emil. Have you played soccer before?"

He looked at me and responded with a snappy "Meow."

Startled, my brain struggled to process what he said, and I turned to his awkwardly smiling parents for clarification, but they offered nothing. I attempted to defuse the tension with a generic follow-up question.

"Are you ready to play?"

"Meow, meow," was his response, as if it was customary to converse in that fashion.

Still confused but with an inkling of what was transpiring, I defaulted to the common language of soccer, "Okay, grab a ball and join your teammates."

I felt relief when Emil did as I suggested, but the language barrier remained. After that conversation, Emil meowed his affirmation whenever I gave him instructions or a position assignment. It took some getting used to. One meow meant "no," two "yes,"—I think. He was a capable player who spoke English well, but at soccer, he spoke cat.

Our returning players were a welcome contrast to the newcomers. Those six girls and two boys, all with two years of soccer under their belts, were ready to take their game to the next level. It was an exciting challenge.

AT OUR SECOND practice, Megan's team chose "Tigers" as their name, and we started establishing a routine. I ability-grouped players to manage a broad range of talent. I introduced the day's skill to the experienced players and then passed them off to Coach Paul. While he reinforced the lesson, I schooled the new players, emphasizing the fundamentals of kicking, passing, and shooting. After a few practices, we merged the groups, and our team began to coalesce.

Things had changed since Wade played U7, and 4v4 soccer was an adjustment for me. Teams in the league were expected to field two groups of four individuals on each game day. The two teams played simultaneously, with extra players substituting as the game proceeded. The goals were tiny, only about as wide as the span of an adult's arms from fingertip to fingertip, and there were no goalkeepers. Players were not supposed to stand before a goal to defend it but to mark opponents or attack. The pitches were small because the theory was that a confined area kept players more involved with more opportunities to touch the ball. Games were regulated by a parent or coach from each team who refereed together—that usually worked if the adults behaved. Occasionally, there was a problem because some players, like Jacob, couldn't control their urge to stand in the goal. After being reminded to play the ball, they would run to the goal, guard it exclusively, or hang on it—all unacceptable. That behavior raised the ire of opposing coaches, who reminded me, "No goalkeepers." There was nothing I could say or do short of going onto the field and moving the player away from the goal.

Playing two games simultaneously felt like structured chaos. I assigned Paul one team, and I took the other. Then we both waded off into a sea of shouting wannabe-coach parents and did our best. The games went fast, with four ten-minute quarters. When they were over, the entire team rendezvoused at the gear bag for a snack and juice before dispersing. Paul and I would confer, feeling dazed by all the activity, and discuss how the day went, then do it again the following week.

Our season went well, and time flew by. It felt like I was always preparing for the next soccer thing because I was coaching two teams, and the pace of Megan's practices and games was fast. The girls on her team were solid and reliable. They were prone to discussions of how their undershirt complemented the color of their jersey, and they were not as aggressive as the boys, but they were team players.

Our boys were a mixture; some were odd, some were great, and some were strongly influenced by their dads, who thought they were potential superstars. Superstars were frustrating. They didn't listen to me, especially during games, because their dads stood on the sideline and encouraged them to play in ways that made them stand out. Our fields were small; it was easy for a dad to command his player's attention and ensure that my advice to pass to an open teammate was ignored. Often, dads encouraged classic, if not flamboyant, soccer moves or tricks to beat defenders. The problem was that the dads lacked the knowledge or skill to teach effectively, and their expectations exceeded their offsprings' abilities. An essential aspect of any soccer move is an emphasis on accelerating away to escape with the ball. However, most dads who attempted to teach an escape move emphasized footwork with the ball and forgot the subtle importance of breaking away. Consequently, superstars often failed on the field. They were stymied as one, two, and sometimes three defenders surrounded them while they high-stepped over the ball, executing an ineffective Irish jig that didn't ward off or fool the most basic defenders. The outcome was always the same. The ball was lost to our opponent, and I dealt with a brainwashed individual who refused to be a team player. Fortunately, the superstar phenomenon only mattered in close games when teamwork was essential, and we didn't have many of those.

Our best players were evenly split: three boys and three girls, and Megan was one of them. She scored her first goal that season. Somehow, Judy managed to snap a picture of the aftermath as Megan walked away from the net with a bounce in her step and the same look on her face that she had at age two, which said: "See, told you I could do it." It was one of the first bricks of what would become an amazing tower of confidence.

MIDWAY THROUGH THE season, I experienced my first and only emergency room visit with a player. The event began during warm-up. Jacob said he didn't want to play because his throat felt funny. He looked fine. I assumed he was getting a cold or was overwhelmed and needed a break, so I told him to sit on the bleachers near us and return when he was ready. About ten minutes later, I realized he had not returned. I found him still on the bleachers but with his back to the field. He was propped up on his hands on the back row as if doing a pushup; I thought he was playing and went to get him down so he didn't fall. As I walked around the back of the bleachers to face him, I realized that he was crying, fidgeting uncomfortably back and forth on his hands, and staring at the parking lot.

I asked what was wrong, and he grasped his throat with both hands and managed a garbled, "My noat hurts. My nongue feels funny."

I stared at him, wondering, *What is happening with this kid?* Then it hit me: *Anaphylaxis! His tongue was swelling, and his throat was closing up.* I assessed him carefully; he was talking, his color was good, and he was breathing normally. I concluded I had a little time. I picked him up and ran over to Paul, "Jacob's having an allergic reaction; you're in charge. I'm taking him to the emergency room."

Halfway to the parking lot, my thought process was, *Call his mom. Where's her number? Medical release form. Go back to the gear bag.*

I was sure the forms were there. I kept them in a plastic bag with the worthless player passes. I carried them everywhere for years, and it seemed like they were constantly in the way. They were always there, ALWAYS, unless it had rained at the last game and all the paperwork had gotten wet, then they were spread out on my bedroom floor. I rifled through the bag for about ten seconds before I remembered where the releases were, then I grabbed Jacob and headed to the parking lot for the three-minute drive to my house.

When I got there, I found Judy at home. I sat Jacob at our kitchen table and told her what was happening; she watched him while I located the form. When I returned, she had worked her mom magic—he looked calmer and less stressed but still complained of an itchy "noat." I phoned his mom— no answer. I thought hard. I didn't know what to do. Someone had to contact his mom at the soccer field after practice, and I was the only one who knew what she looked like; someone else had to take him to the emergency room just in case. Judy drew the short straw. I buckled Jacob into the back seat of her minivan, gave her the paperwork, and sent her to the hospital. Then, I returned to the soccer field and waited for his mom. It was a long twenty minutes, made longer because she arrived late. She was surprisingly calm as I approached without Jacob and told her where he was.

The hospital was only about a mile away and was my next stop. I found Judy there, still in Emergency, exerting a calming influence, but the show was over. Because she had the medical release, the hospital staff responded quickly and administered an injection to relieve Jacob's symptoms.

When his mom arrived, Jacob was propped up in a bed, looking alert and comfortable. It seemed like our response had been an overreaction. She nodded to Judy but didn't say a word to her or me. I expected her to rush to Jacob's side in a flurry of relief, but she looked more annoyed than alarmed and stood back with her coat folded over her crossed arms as she waited for the doctor to return. Judy and I excused our-selves. I went home and changed my underwear.

After dinner, Judy broke the bad news that she reserved for the right moment, "I hate to tell you this after what you've just been through, but … Jacob barfed all over the back of the van." She unconsciously micro-expressed a look of dis-gust, then shook it off with a shrug and a shiver. I hung my head, took a deep breath, and went to the garage to inspect the damage. I spent the next hour cleaning half-digested, mucous-encrusted peanuts from the floor of the van as well as the compartment below the floor designed to receive the fold-down seats, mumbling and cursing while I worked, ask-ing myself when I would see the big money that made it all worthwhile.

THE SUCCESS OF the Tigers was welcome after the strug-gles of Wade's team, but the effects of too much competition on human nature often destroyed what should have been a fun experience. After one game, as I collected my thoughts and equipment on the sideline, I witnessed an interaction that evoked deep sympathy for a player and left me shaking my head at the misguided way some adults approach their child's soccer experience. It involved a player on the opposing team who was a crack shot. He was a quick little guy with a strong right leg, great aim, and the ability to put the ball in the goal almost from the center line. His team demolished us, and he led the attack. He was the attack—a one-kid team. He waited on the field when the game ended while other players departed with their parents. Finally, his mom appeared, and he ran to her, shouting excitedly, "We won, Mommy."

Her response was gruff and demeaning, "What was the score?"

The kid's attitude changed instantly from happy to crestfallen and intimidated. "I don't know," he admitted.

"Well, ask the referee," she ordered.

Who cares? I thought. The "referee" was a random parent who probably didn't keep track. Her kid had played brilliantly; she should have given him a high-five and a hug. Her behavior confounded me because she ignored his successful use of new skills and failed to recognize his effort so he would be motivated to continue. She focused only on the score, and unless she planned to reward him for every goal, she made an unimportant aspect of the game the highlight for her six-year-old son.

AS OUR SEASON ended, we wanted to do something special to celebrate our successful start as a team. Judy surveyed parents, and the consensus was that it would be fun to do T-shirts. Once again, I searched the internet for content and settled on a black-and-white line drawing of a sleepy-looking Bengal tiger. I arranged each player's name underneath the image and the word "Tigers" over the top. Judy ordered the production of twelve T-shirts, and we handed them out at the recognition ceremony after our last game.

Then, before the team went home for the winter, I had them huddle one last time. I knelt and extended my arm with a closed fist.

"Everybody in," I said.

The team knew what to do and closed around me with their hands on top of mine.

"Tigers on three. One, two, three ..." I shouted.

The response was a thunderous chorus of eleven "Tigers" and one "Meow."

Chapter 49

Accolades for the Purples

THAT WINTER, OWEN and I spent several blustery Saturdays in December and January driving frozen roads so he could participate in an "international" indoor soccer tournament. There was no explanation of what was international about the competition. Teams were not required to have rosters comprising individuals of different nationalities, no colorful flags of the world decorated the gym, and the audience was not divided into nationalistic sections of boisterous fans challenging each other with raucous cheers.

Indoor soccer facilities are enormous establishments that charge a fee for access and often are not centrally located. To compete, players need time, money, and someone with the wherewithal to transport them. I suspected that the international promotion was intended to entice players from racial minorities to the facility and expand its appeal beyond the usual audience.

Owen's team took the bait. The core of his company was two brothers and a cousin, all of whom immigrated from Mexico. The three organized the lineup using their friends and family, except for Owen, whom they had come to know in high school soccer. Owen leveraged his Spanish curriculum and skill with the ball, and the group played well together. One by one, the other not-so-international squads fell to Owen's, and on the last Saturday in January, his team hoisted the trophy above their heads. It seemed like they had the nucleus of a group that would do well in high school. But despite their success, we never saw most of the international team again because, as sophomores in high school with access to a car, they all got jobs that conflicted with practices and games. It was the beginning of the end of Owen's formal soccer-playing days.

IN FEBRUARY, I attended our league's annual soccer meeting. In contrast to our club gatherings, the league meeting was held in a banquet hall and attended by officers and representatives from all the clubs. Each group sat at its table and shared dinner before the business meeting and awards. Some participants loved the event. I hated it because I wasn't motivated by acclaim or league expansion. It was my third trip to the meeting and my second time winning our club's Coach of the Year. I embarrassed myself on the previous occasion when I was vice president because I had suggested that I didn't need to attend the meeting.

"Couldn't someone just take notes so we all don't need to go?" I asked.

What I didn't know was that our club president was trying to surprise me with the award at the meeting, a fact that he grudgingly revealed to coerce me to attend. It was an awkward interaction, so on the second occasion, I didn't protest.

When I arrived, I chatted and ate my dinner, received

my award, and then patiently waited for the end—until something got my attention. With great fanfare, one of the delegations announced that one of their coaches had led a team from our league to a tournament championship in Florida and won! The announcement was met with enthusiastic applause from everyone but me because I knew the coach and the team well: they were the Purples. It was hard not to clap. Surrounded by a room full of spontaneous applause, the social animal in me wanted to do what everyone else was doing. But my self-respect wouldn't allow it to continue. I stopped myself as the realization of what I was celebrating jelled in my consciousness.

I understood why the audience was clapping because the achievement sounded great. The Purples had attained the ultimate accomplishment from the perspective of soccer zealots and small-town coaches who were not satisfied playing in the local rec league. The Purples had fought it out with the big boys in the big league and won. But I felt no satisfaction having coached a team that they steamrolled twice yearly just because they needed a sparring partner. I was angry. They bent the rules and pitted their select group against average rec teams in the area because there was no one else to play. They got away with it because the soccer zealots in charge permitted it, while the rest of us were ignorant or unsure of what recourse was available. Their success came at the expense of others. Even after that night, we played them once or twice more before our time as Timberwolves was done. They embarrassed us, crushed our self-esteem, and always made us do the Losers' Walk.

Chapter 50

Plan B

IN SPRING, I turned the crank again. Paul and I coached the Tigers to a positive winning season; Bob and I coached the Timberwolves to another character-building season. At the end of it all, I faced the prospect of struggling with Wade's team for one more year. In my mind, the struggle could be avoided, so I wrote a letter to Henry, the club president, whom I knew well because he had been Owen's coach. That was the time, I argued, to dissolve our combined-age team and move *en masse* to another soccer program because the season was over. I wanted to make a decision quickly so we could get the word out for all the players to register in the new program—no man left behind. I knew Henry understood our struggle. I also knew I could trust him not to blow the issue out of proportion.

In two pages, I laid out the problems and the potential solutions of my Plan B to combine forces with the neighboring soccer program. I detailed how both struggling clubs would benefit and how the move would help girls and boys in the U11, U12, U13, and U14 age brackets. All the age groups for both genders could play in their respective divisions. I emphasized that I wasn't suggesting scrapping our local program, just combining when it made sense. Lastly, I said we should resist the tendency to fight change because of civic pride. There was no shame in trying to do what was best for our kids so they could enjoy a better experience. I was open to discussion, and I at least wanted to talk about it.

I never got a response. Two weeks later, I saw Henry and inquired if he had received my letter. He confirmed that he had but didn't say more. I couldn't blame him for not wanting to paint a target on his forehead. We lived in a small town. Some people would have hated the proposal, and he had to earn a living. Despite my misgivings and lacking a blessing or even a thoughtful conversation, I didn't do anything more. Diplomacy was never my strong suit, and even after eight years, I still felt like the Beers were perceived as outsiders who had moved to town from the big city. Doomed by inaction, Wade and I pushed on one last time.

Chapter 51

Year 11–End of
the Timberwolves

THAT FALL, THE struggle with Wade's team was one of my life's most mentally difficult and frustrating challenges. Neither the team nor I gave up, but we were not competitive. Since wins were elusive, I told myself to take a long-term view and consider my efforts as a contribution to a successful high school experience. I came to practices with new drills, workouts, and high expectations, but we were outgunned.

To avoid injury, I occasionally told opposing coaches that they were competing against a combined team of sixth-, seventh-, and eighth-grade players. I wasn't begging for mercy; I intended to protect our smaller players from overly enthusiastic, more-mature adversaries. It seemed to work because even the Purples cut us some slack. Still, our opponents shut us out, and we never scored a goal. It wasn't fun.

Our numbers had dwindled to the point where we couldn't field a team. I solved the problem by inviting two of the girls to return. They were playing in their division. Nothing prevented them from participating on our team because it was officially coed. They jumped at the opportunity to rejoin, and the older boys who remembered them didn't mind. Having the girls at games and practices made our challenge feel more like a joint effort, as if everyone was pitching in to achieve a common purpose, and a little spark returned.

Halfway through the season, the Friendly Tournament was an issue. The girls had their own game that day, and several boys had somewhere else to be, so I told our club president that we would not attend because I couldn't field a team. A few days later, I got a call from the league president scolding me for not participating. I explained our situation, but his argument kept circling back to my obligation. It was a short conversation. He was a soccer zealot, and his assertions were about rules, not the reality that we did not have enough players to make a team on tournament day.

Our last practice, Gator Day, was great fun. We warmed up, stretched, and played a minigame, then took a break and broke into the cooler. There were some surplus Gatorades that I brought to avoid conflicts over flavors. Always cautious, I remembered the Gator Day all those years ago when Drew had drunk two and spewed them over the soccer field, but there was no need to worry—this group was more mature, and no player begged for more. We had struggled and bled together for a common goal. On that afternoon, everyone was satisfied with what they had.

The following weekend, we were short players for our match. We had just enough, eleven, if Wade played with a 102-degree fever. He and I discussed his status, and ultimately, Wade took one for the team. He was pretty droopy, but a congested, lethargic Wade was at least dependable. I put him in the goal for the entire game, and he made it through without mishap. There was no plan for a celebration afterward. We had experienced a disappointing season, and spring was in our future, so it seemed appropriate to postpone the ceremony. Still, the last game was an opportunity to have a team meeting, and I debated with myself about how to handle our situation. I wanted to broach the subject of dissolving the team, but it didn't seem right to do it at that time and location while the opposing team looked on, and I was afraid that people wouldn't comprehend the whole story.

I had everyone's mailing address, so after discussing the situation with Wade, I decided to plead my case to players and parents via snail mail. I drafted a letter that described how our soccer club had always adopted a philosophy of self-determination, composing a program using what was available in our community, but I argued that continuing that approach was not our team's best action plan. I offered several alternatives and advocated for combining with the other soccer club because it was the best solution for our boys and girls. I asked parents and players to inform our club president or me of their preferred solution. Then I sealed those envelopes, dropped them in the mail, and waited to hear.

Weeks went by, then months. Finally, in February, Ben's dad called me. Ben had decided to do as I recommended and join the other club. It was a death blow to our team because, without Ben, we didn't have a prayer. In that instant, the Timberwolves winked out of existence. We talked briefly. I assured him I understood, wished him good luck, and ended the call. I wasn't surprised; I had essentially given permission for players to do what Ben did. Deep down, I was glad it was over.

The next day, I called our club president and told him

that because of Ben's withdrawal, I was no longer interested in trying to keep the team together. We discussed the range of ages on the team, my concerns about younger players getting hurt, and how difficult it was to motivate players confronted by stronger teams every week. I thought Wade and some other players weren't having fun but remained committed to the team. In my judgment, that didn't seem fair, so I was calling an end to it. President Henry didn't argue and was probably relieved as well.

I watched both of my sons' rec soccer teams follow the same trajectory toward disintegration. While the boys endured the experience, they certainly hadn't thrived. There had to be something better. Unfortunately, the community was unwilling to change. I swore I would not let Megan's team descend the same death spiral.

Chapter 52

Wade's Evolution

WADE'S SOCCER EXPERIENCE ended without a singular, spectacular day where he transformed before my eyes as there had been for Owen. Like his older brother, Wade had developed into a skilled player, but circumstances that showcased his ability didn't occur. Instead, I watched as he embraced my advice and pushed himself to do all sorts of athletic things. In high school, he participated in football, cross country, track, baseball, and tennis. He worked out in the gym with Owen, and taught himself to swim a mile in open water to participate in a local triathlon where he finished first in class. He developed a reputation in our family for being fearless and willing to endure unknown risks to experience something new. He accomplished everything that Judy and I had hoped for and more. I couldn't have been prouder.

Chapter 53

Owen's Last Soccer Season

OWEN'S FALL SOCCER season mirrored Wade's—disappointment. The high-school coach he liked so much, and who the team flourished under so well, resigned. The new coach was quiet and uninspiring. He knew soccer but was unemotional and businesslike—there was no X-factor. Owen soldiered on, hoping that the coach was just different, and that things would improve after an adjustment period—they didn't. The new coach failed to communicate with his players and never inquired about their preferred positions. Instead, he assigned roles based on his perception of player skill and got it wrong. He moved Owen forward to a position he disliked, and other players were also out of their comfort zones.

The team also struggled with the gradual withdrawal of Hispanic players. They attended preseason practices because, at 6 a.m., no player had a conflict with work. That changed once school started because after-school employment and soccer conflicted. It took a week or two, but one by one, the boys with jobs gave up trying to juggle both activities. The turmoil continued for half the season until his coach finally asked players what positions they favored, then rebuked them for not speaking sooner. At least he wasn't inflexible. He adjusted the lineup, and the team started to play better, but by then, a frustrated Owen was done with the coach and high-school soccer.

Faced with the departure of his friends and a coach who didn't motivate him, Owen finished the season and decided to try something he always wanted to do—play halfback on an American football team. I was sorry to see his soccer exploits end, but I understood.

Owen's last games were fun because he was back in his old position. He routinely worked magic, breaking up attacks and accelerating away with the ball, his oversized shirt flowing in the wind as he ran. His movements were natural and fluid, catching other teams off guard. Before they could react and converge, he passed the ball to teammates who pressed the attack. Those moments of excellence earned knowing nods of gratitude from teammates and burned the memory of his ability into my brain.

Chapter 54

Success for Megan's Team

IN CONTRAST TO the boys, Megan's fall soccer experience went well. She emerged as a determined defender and a capable goalkeeper. Her competitive spirit and experiences growing up with two older brothers made her supremely confident. A goal or a larger player never rattled her. Her quick reflexes gave her an advantage over others because she had the ability to move and recover before opponents could react. If she struggled, it was because she decided to grow her hair longer, and her bangs were an awkward length—too short to be captured by a headband, yet long enough that they interfered with her vision no matter how far back she tipped her head. For a few weeks in the heart of soccer season, I was frustrated when she blundered because hair was in her eyes. Neither she nor Judy could find a solution, and although I threatened to deploy athletic tape, I was powerless to effect change.

That fall, the team advanced to a larger field. We lost the boy who spoke cat but gained a set of fraternal twins, a girl named Alexa, and a boy, Aiden. The twins were small for their age and lacked experience playing soccer, but they came from athletic parents, and those genes ran true. They were gifted athletes and overcame deficits in ability with hard work and curious exchanges where they huddled together, conversing in what appeared to be a silent language that ultimately evoked a nod of understanding.

Alexa was a standout. Some players do more than run and dribble the ball—they flow, lengthening, not shortening their stride to get their steps right in a fluid motion with graceful perfection. I saw her move that way at our first game on a sun-baked, rock-hard grade school playground pockmarked with bumps and bare spots that made the ball bounce unpredictably. We faced a team that wore red and white uniforms from a larger community than ours. I feared being overwhelmed by an adversary with greater depth and more competitive experience. We trailed by a point when she received a well-timed pass on the run at midfield. Two defenders moved to block her path to the goal and formed a defensive wall. Alexa instinctively split the half-hearted defense and kicked the ball between them. The defenders watched as the ball shot past, followed by Alexa, who accelerated and glided through the gap on her way to the goal.

Coaching her was confusing because while she was new to the game, her ability was light years ahead of me. I didn't treat her any differently than other players. The best I could do was to offer suggestions and provide an opportunity for her to teach herself and then be amazed when she did something beyond what I taught. When I talked, she listened; when I demonstrated, she absorbed and interpreted what she learned into her dialect. She was left-footed, I was right; she was young and nimble, I, old and cumbersome. Nothing I taught looked the same after she translated it. She wasn't shy but was humble and never flaunted her ability or sought the limelight. That was her only weakness: she was too polite. When she snatched the ball from an opponent, she frequently offered a sincere "Sorry" over her shoulder as she darted away as if she was aware that her success came at the expense of her opponent. Still, if a game was close, I could always rely on her to do her best to fill a gap in our defense or advance our attack—silent support. I had to guard against overusing her because, as a coach, I wanted to throw her at every tough challenge that confronted us.

Coaching Alexa inspired me because I witnessed her accomplishments firsthand and felt that, in some way, I played a part. She was amazing to watch, and her actions evoked an odd thought—if I were a hunter-gatherer relying on the physical ability of my clan for survival, she was the person I'd want in my tribe, and we had her.

We were thirteen players—eight girls and five boys—and we were awesome. The boys contributed aggression; the girls brought patience and teamwork. The strengths of both genders seemed to rub off on the other, generating mutual respect. After being together for years, the team played without internal disputes and trusted one another. All of our games were competitive. That experience was a more balanced struggle than I had been through with Wade's crew, and it was easy to stay positive.

Chapter 55

Executive Decision

WHEN MY CHILDREN did homework and slogged through a tedious assignment, I did what I could to help, then encouraged them by saying, "It's essential to keep working because if you can get a little bit ahead of the rest of the class, you will have an advantage in the future. The next time you encounter the material, you will absorb more than your classmates and extend your advantage. You will be ahead of the curve, and life will be easier."

That was happening to Megan's team. They were above average, and it was up to me to ensure they stayed there. I knew the transition to all-boys teams was looming, and I could see it already. I also knew that game formats would grow; 6v6 would advance to 8v8 and 11v11. Football would conflict with soccer in the fall, resulting in player shortages.

The player's job was to do their best on the field; my job was to help them accomplish that and avoid turbulent waters stirred by civic pride. I knew the death spiral that haunted our soccer club couldn't be avoided because I had lived the corroborating history. I also suspected some people wouldn't like my solution to abandon our local soccer club for a slightly more successful one in a neighboring community. There was no way for Megan to avoid the death spiral without destroying the local team because she was a vital participant, and I was their coach. If we joined another club, I suspected others would follow, gutting the home team and eliminating it from successive ranks for years. Nevertheless, I planned to ignore what others thought and do what was in the players' best interests. If people didn't like that, I would take the heat because it was the best option for my daughter and her teammates.

Chapter 56

Lean and Mean

THREE PLAYERS DIDN'T return to Megan's team in the spring. One was a girl who lost interest, one was a superstar lost to an elite club, and the third was Jacob. I never learned what happened to him. I wasn't sorry to see him go. The experience of cleaning vomit out of Judy's van probably tainted my feelings. He wasn't badly behaved, just unfocused.

Teammates like him negatively influenced our performance during games and sometimes were worse than playing short-handed. At least when we were down a player, we compensated by redistributing responsibilities. But when an unfocused individual was on the field, the team depended on them to do a job; when they failed because of a lack of concentration or weak skills, our opponents gained an immediate advantage. It was incredibly frustrating, even embarrassing, to watch a slippery opponent break away with the ball and make a beeline toward our goal, defended by our keeper and an inattentive player whose responsibility was to challenge the attacker and stall them until help arrived. I did what I could to help from the sideline by shouting with hands cupped around my mouth to make my voice carry.

"Be ready. Challenge and wait for the mistake."

Then I watched helplessly as my defender, *my responsibility*, stood flat-footed and failed to act, leaving his comrade susceptible to a demoralizing goal.

I spent significant one-on-one time working with unfocused players, trying to make them capable so they wouldn't be a source of discord. I organized breakout sessions with the target players and a few others who needed refreshing. In those sessions, I emphasized proper form and then drilled it in, attempting to make the behavior automatic so that even unfocused players had the correct response to challenging situations. Usually, my efforts yielded good results. Weak players were never great, but most became useful defenders, contributed, and got stronger. My motivation was selfish. I knew we would be desperate for players and couldn't afford to let a potential contributor with unrealized talent languish.

Without Jacob and the other two players, we were a lean but capable ten, and I focused on improving the team. I suspected our season and the subsequent fall and spring would be easy. After the struggle I had been through with Wade, I knew I was fortunate. All the pieces were falling into place. First, Megan's team was well-trained and had been together for years, so there were no challenging skill deficits to overcome. Second, no select teams or referees bent the rules in our division. Lastly, the soccer clinics I attended were paying off. I taught the same material I employed with Wade's group, but more effectively.

Despite our experiences, the team and I still had much to learn. Most games revealed weaknesses I addressed at subsequent practices with tailor-made drills scoured from clinics and the internet. In general, Coach Paul and I solved problems as they came up and let players play. The weeks of practice and competitive games went fast.

Chapter 57

Year 12–Turtles

OUR SUCCESS CULMINATED a year later with an away game on the last day of the spring season, the day we played the all-boys Footballers. We called ourselves the Turtles. Megan was in the fourth grade, the same as Wade when his team experienced its Golden Season.

It was unseasonably hot for mid-May, almost 90 degrees. I brought water in an orange five-gallon insulated cooler to counteract the effects of the heat. I planned to use it to fill bottles and douse players' heads to keep them fresh. Our competition was a group of boys who played American football together in the fall and soccer in the spring to stay in shape. I knew they would be disciplined from their time together, but they weren't a select soccer team. That fact made me confident that we had an excellent chance to defeat them. So, I was excited and intense and tried to evoke the same from the Turtles, who looked a little overwhelmed at the thought of playing in the heat.

When we huddled before the game, I tried to rally the team and calm their fears of playing the bulging Footballers.

"They feel the heat, too," I reminded the team. "And

they are not soccer players. Play our game, make good passes, control the ball, and have fun."

Then I sent six players out onto the pitch.

As the teams took the field, there was a noticeable difference in player size. Megan was short for her age, in the fifth percentile for height, and only one of the twins, Aiden, was smaller. Judy and I suspected that her steroid-based asthma medicine was slowing her growth. Under her doctor's supervision, we weaned her off the medication, but she had not experienced a growth spurt. Sending someone like that onto the field against a football team gave me pause, but if it bothered Megan or anyone else, they didn't let on. Instead, they fearlessly went out and played hard.

Unlike football, soccer does not reward a player's size. Great size or strength is not necessarily an advantage because those things can be countered with speed, agility, and skill with the ball. In addition, rules about possession of the ball mitigate player interactions—although both players have a right to the ball, blatant pushing by contesting players is not allowed. They must play the ball, not the opponent. Referees are responsible for managing interactions on the field; if things get rough, they call a foul for charging or dangerous play. If Megan and her teammates had faith in anything that day, it was that the referee would protect them; their experience taught them that. To the Footballers' credit, the ref didn't need to act beyond keeping time and normal game regulation.

By halftime, we led 2-1. As our red-faced team came off the field, I prioritized ensuring everyone had water. Paul and the twins' dad filled water bottles and dispensed Soakers (water poured over the head) to any player who wanted one. My next priority was to assess player condition. Everyone seemed okay. The team was mostly silent, resting, taking the occasional sip of water. I grew concerned that they were going flat. With a minute of halftime remaining, I refocused the team's attention.

"On your feet and loosen up."

Players took a last sip and then began stretching. I waited for the referee's whistle to call us back to the field; then we huddled one last time.

"Be ready to play at the start," I urged. "Don't get caught hot and tired. Be patient on defense, wait for the mistake, fight balls off to the side, then up the line, get your head up, and make good passes."

I had their attention now.

"Twenty-five minutes of soccer to go. We've had a great season. Go out and finish it off."

I extended my arm and closed fist and waited a moment.

"Turtles on three! One, two, three!"

Midway through the half, the Footballers tied the game 2-2. I didn't change anything except substitute players who were tired. It was hot, and we were playing well; there was no point in fixing what wasn't broken. The Footballers kept the pressure on. I suspected their coach had made an adjustment and changed a player assignment to increase their attack. That change left them weaker on defense and was a fatal decision. With two minutes to go, the Footballers were near our goal; Alexa was back, helping our keeper when she intercepted the ball and dribbled it out of the middle, straight to the sideline where her brother waited. She made a crisp pass and Aiden a solid trap before he accelerated away. Angry Footballers began to converge, so he cleared the ball up the line.

The ball shot past Marge at midfield. She was new to the

team that spring. She played soccer before joining us and had four siblings, all close to her age, so she got lots of practice. Marge charged after the ball but could manage only an exhausted ramble. She was fast enough and stopped the ball just before it rolled off the field. The speed of the clear kick and Marge's pursuit of the ball created space. No defender was near her. She labored, turned her body, and began to dribble toward the goal. As she did, she saw Coach Paul's son, John, closing from midfield.

Marge settled herself, then passed. That instant was the goalkeeper's chance. He should have charged out and scooped up the ball, but he didn't. Instead, John and the ball arrived at the middle of the penalty box simultaneously. He trapped it, then stepped and kicked.

The keeper wasn't fast enough to match the speed of Marge's pass, so half the goal was open for John. He and his teammates scored the winning goal with a minute remaining, and a cheer went up on the parents' sideline. Our sideline cheered, too, especially the dads. The clock ticked while players congratulated John, and two exhausted teams lined up for one more kickoff. I watched concerned, leery of a letdown and a freak quick goal, but time elapsed, and the referee signaled an end to the game.

It was a great win. Elated, I high-fived every player and coach on our sideline. What was remarkable about the contest was not that our undersized team defeated the Footballers, but that we played as a team so well at the end. It was a great combination of player ability, teamwork, and self-control while faced with tremendous pressure. I was so proud of how the team played. I wished it could end like a storybook right then, but I had more to do. I waited until the celebrating subsided and the juice boxes and snack bars were consumed. Then, before the players departed, I called a team meeting.

I did everything opposite to what I did with Wade's team. I held the meeting on the field where others could observe. I didn't provide notice or documentation. I explained what would happen to the team in the future as football siphoned off boys, and the number of players required on the field increased from six to eight and, ultimately, eleven. As evidence of the trends, I pointed out that we had one boy who had already made clear his intention to play football and one girl who would be playing volleyball. The alternative I offered was to dissolve the team and migrate to the neighboring soccer club so boys and girls could play in their own divisions.

It was a bitter pill for Coach Paul. He was having fun and couldn't reconcile our successful day with the bad news I delivered. He argued desperately to find a way to keep the team together, but I countered that there was no way. I was unwavering because the trends were unavoidable. We had to break up to succeed in the future. My last words were, "You're free to do what you want, but Megan and I will go to the other team this fall." I hoped they would trust me and follow. All the girls and most boys did.

It was a sad way to end the day but necessary because our migration to the other club was the best option and one of my best decisions. Instead of being a little fish in a big ocean of all-boys teams, Megan and I would be part of a team that was at least a typical fish in an all-girls pond. That parity held promise for our future. Good things always come to an end, and my last act as coach of the Turtles was to dissolve the team. I ended it because I was trying to ensure that good things would continue to happen for everyone in the future.

Chapter 58

Year 13–Turtle Migration

THE PRESIDENT OF the neighboring soccer club was a woman, Gail, who happened to be the coach of Owen's tournament team. Gail was aware that I had coached Wade's and Megan's teams. Consequently, I was hopeful when I checked the box on Megan's registration form that asked if I was willing to coach her team. Weeks passed. Finally, around the first of August, I got a call inviting me to attend the coaches' meeting at the home field. I arrived to find Gail and a soccerish-looking group of parents seated at picnic tables in the park's pavilion. Gail welcomed me and presented my coach's binder. After a few opening remarks, Gail handed the meeting over to Janet, who was the coach of girls' soccer at the high school.

Coach Janet had a peculiar way of public speaking. She used one voice when involved in everyday conversation and an oddly commanding voice in front of a small audience of adult coaches. Many people get anxious when they talk in front of a crowd, so I tried not to judge because I didn't know her, but there seemed to be more to her tone and exaggerated movements than nervousness. As she continued, I realized her authoritarian mannerisms weren't my imagination; she was a soccer zealot. Janet's expectations took a demanding turn when she began lecturing about managing the parents' meeting. She advised coaches to ask for a volunteer to be "Team Mom," the official liaison to the team. If I needed something done, I was to communicate it to the Team Mom, and she was supposed to take care of it. That sounded great, but I knew that having an unnecessary chain of command was fraught with potential for miscommunication.

Coach Janet had a long list of responsibilities that needed to be assigned. Most were unrealistic because parents did not want to videotape games, fundraise, or market soccer club swag. And, in a sexist twist, I was offended by the title Team Mom because I had previously mastered all the responsibilities. What if the Team Mom was a dad like me? Did I still have to call him the Team Mom? Were the Team Mom and Dad supposed to marry and have a Team Baby? What if they were first cousins? It was all so complicated and unnecessary.

Eventually, the lecture about delegating authority to the Team Mom responsible for finding volunteers to meet unrealistic expectations ended. I took my soccer gear and got out of there because I had wasted another quiet August evening listening to ridiculous rules.

When I got home, I was welcomed by Judy, who asked, "How did the meeting go?"

She expected me to shake my head in aggravation like always. It was our ritual and her way of helping me forget the meeting and move on. However, I surprised her with an unusual display of enthusiasm. I smiled and exuberantly thrust my roster over my head.

"All the Turtles migrated together," I beamed. "And I'm

the coach of the girls U11 team. We're one big happy turtle family, and I'm their mom!"

Chapter 59

New Team, New Challenges

THE SOCCER CLUB we joined was like our old one: small and rural. However, it was part of a community with a union high school; consequently, it attracted players from several municipalities and had the word "United" in its name. I hoped the motivation behind the phrase was genuine because the Turtles and United would be teammates for years.

I planned a normal routine for our first practice: warmup, stretch, review a skill, and conclude with a game, but there were some surprises. The practice field was a long way from the parking lot. It was too far, I thought, to expect parents to go, so I loitered near the drop-off area, waiting to see if anyone had questions for me—no one stopped to talk. I was surprised that parents were comfortable leaving their daughters with some strange man at a remote park with no one else around. As the traffic dwindled, it dawned on me that there would not be any questions, charging lionesses, or first-time soccer parents without a clue. They were experienced parents who were glad they didn't need to coach their child's team. With that realization, I abandoned my post in the parking lot and started practice.

I didn't want differences to divide our combined team,

so I intentionally made the afternoon fun and fast-paced. I suspected that Megan and her Turtle teammates were apprehensive about joining a new group. Fortunately, they comprised one-third of the team, providing more than a glimmer of familiarity. In contrast, the United girls probably viewed us as interlopers—the new players who didn't belong. Those divisions were blurred by my dual status as an outsider and new coach as I warmed up the team with a dribbling exercise. To prevent girls from bunching up into cliques, I minimized slack time to force them to interact through the game of soccer. I didn't know that the team had many more divisions than Turtles and United. There were rich and poor players, popular and anonymous ones, seasoned athletes and beginners, as well as those accustomed and unaccustomed to equal responsibility on the soccer field. There were so many divisions that almost all the girls were anxious—a clean slate. Consequently, practice went well. We got through dribbling and passing; then, I did something that produced a remarkable outcome.

I knew tightening the defense was one of the most productive ways to improve a new team. I wanted to introduce the concept early and proceeded with the familiar defender drill. I arranged girls in two opposing lines. In turn, the first girl in each queue advanced to a set of cones forming a gate. To win, the player with a ball had to dribble through the cones and maintain possession; her opponent, the defender, had to stop the advance by taking possession or kicking the ball away. The girls took turns until the last pair stood first in line. One was Megan, and the other was the largest girl on the team—a big, boisterous girl who was head and shoulders taller than Megan and almost twice her weight. The size disparity was comical—at least twelve inches, one-quarter of Megan's total height. It was David and Goliath, and all eyes were on the battlefield.

The two competitors appraised each other for a tense few seconds as they waited at their starting spots. I was concerned because Megan was so small. She looked dubious as well, but when it was her turn, I paused for only an instant to consider potential outcomes; then I did the same thing I had done for every other pair of competitors and hollered, "Next two."

Goliath moved to the cones at a slow jog, dribbling the ball closely; Megan moved to her spot quickly and waited. The two approached each other, and Goliath faltered. Her instinct was to avoid confrontation and go outside the cones, but the game's rules constrained her. That hesitation was all Megan needed. Without missing a beat, she stepped in, took the ball, turned her back to the girl, and jogged away.

Goliath blushed, threw her hands up, and jeered, "The shrimp got me."

I laughed, not at the shrimp joke, but at the absurdity of two players competing under such ridiculous circumstances and the smaller one coming away with the win. It was a harbinger of things to come. Megan frequently mastered difficult aspects of the game regardless of her stature. She had the strongest leg on the team and perhaps the quickest reactions. The same ability that had helped her excel in gymnastics when she was younger and accomplish dangerous exploits at which her brothers failed, made her a capable soccer player despite her size.

I finished practice that day with a half-field scrimmage. I wanted the girls to have a fun first experience, and they were there to play soccer, so I gave them what they wanted. I used the opportunity to continue my evaluation of players. Near the end of practice, I joined in to see what would happen. Eventually, the ball came to me, and I began to dribble to open space at what I thought was a fast pace when, without warning, Lucy introduced herself. She was an unabashed member of the United team and fast enough to rival even Alexa. She zipped past my left shoulder, stepped in, took the ball, and raced away without touching me. It was a deft move, one that required terrific speed and skill. I stopped in amazement, surprised by Lucy's ability and impressed by her quickness and confidence to be the first girl to challenge a lumbering 200-pound man and take his ball away.

That was enough for one day. I sent the girls home with a schedule and a note asking for someone to act as an assistant coach or at least be available during practice in case of an emergency. After Jacob's allergy attack, I believed in having a second adult present. I was also nervous about the potential for a misunderstanding because I was a man alone with fifteen ten-year-old girls. Fortunately, that was never an issue. Parents would be the issue.

AT THE SECOND practice, a parent named Emily joined us. She was there in response to my plea for an assistant. We chatted for a while about the team, and I asked if she had coached before. She was oddly taciturn and didn't answer, but subtle body language indicated it was a sensitive subject. I didn't have time to analyze her response because I was on a schedule and started practice. What I didn't know, and she didn't tell me, was that she had been the team's coach the previous year and was angry. There had been a mix-up in communication between Emily and Gail, or maybe my assignment as coach was not an accident. Whatever the cause, Emily was not happy being second in command. Every time I helped a player or solved a problem, Emily took it as an insult to her previous coaching efforts. I may have unintentionally offended her frequently with my actions. Each time, it was like twisting a knife in Emily's ribs.

I began our second practice with a quick team meeting and an important message. I told the girls that my coaching philosophy was that everyone got equal playing time. Of course, there were constraints: players had to attend practice and work, but if they did, then no one sat out. Some players, especially the smaller ones, got a wide-eyed look of amazement. One nudged the girl next to her and said something, then they giggled. It was clear that what I said struck a nerve, and as I ordered the girls to their feet, there seemed to be a new enthusiasm for playing.

The opportunity for equal playing time motivated girls who had previously been relegated to the B-team. One seemingly timid whisp of a girl evolved into one of our fastest players, adept at chasing down running attacks; another tall, awkward player blossomed when I taught pushing. Neither girl had the ability or attitude to achieve those things on that second day of practice. They were unassertive, lacking in skills, and resigned to the idea of being bench warmers. By telling them they were expected to play, I gave them responsibility. They knew they had to do a job and began working. It was a simple edict, but I suspected it differed from the previous coach's strategy based on the girls' responses to my announcement. That was the first twist of the knife.

I started from scratch—again. First, the basics of passing and trapping. Many of the girls struggled, and errant soccer balls went everywhere.

"Step and kick," I told them.

Some were embarrassed because there was nowhere to hide. They were paired up, passing back and forth, and it was obvious if they couldn't execute the skill. I used the opportunity to help those who needed it. Most required only minor corrections because they had the physical ability but had never been taught the correct way to pass and trap. It was the same for dribbling and passing on the run, skills the Turtles had learned years prior. Fortunately, the girls were not six years old, so most quickly improved once I took the time to teach a skill.

We scrimmaged for the last fifteen minutes of practice. I roamed the field, regulating the contest, acknowledging smart decisions, and telling players to spread out. Eventually, the ball was kicked off the side of the field. I picked it up and asked, "What do you do for throw-ins?" It was the right question, asked the wrong way. There was a long, silent pause; no one made eye contact, and Coach Emily didn't speak.

Finally, Lucy shrugged, "Nothing" (twist).

I explained the basics of throw-ins, and we scrimmaged for a few more minutes before practice ended. As I walked off the field, the team seemed happy and enthused. Lucy joined me and excitedly released pent-up soccer chatter, loudly proclaiming they had won most of their games the previous year without practicing regularly. Coach Emily was within earshot (twist).

As our first game approached, Emily's daughter, Molly, our goalkeeper, had a weakness that needed attention. When a goalkeeper gets a save, they often dropkick the ball to send it far downfield. When Molly dropkicked, she tossed the ball high into the air and then brought her foot up to meet it, almost at the height of her head; consequently, the ball often traveled straight up, or worse, backward and dangerously close to the goal. I set out to help refine her technique. I taught her the same way I had been taught in high school—hold the ball out at waist level, drop it, then kick. On her first attempt, she struggled and missed.

"Try again," I urged while her mother looked on.

She struck the ball well on the second try, and it sailed downfield. I was surprised that she succeeded so quickly.

"One more." I wanted to confirm her ability wasn't a fluke. She kicked the third ball solidly and harder. I was impressed and congratulated her, offering a high five, which she accepted awkwardly, and then practice moved on.

Competency increased Molly's likelihood of success, gave her confidence, and relieved anxiety, which was good for a goalkeeper. She probably struggled with the skill from her first attempt, maybe for years; I resolved it in about two minutes while her mother and ex-coach looked on (twist).

Chapter 60

Cement Trucks, Sedans
& Porsches

W E LOST OUR first game, but I wasn't disheartened because we were not a cohesive unit, lacked fundamental skills, and our defense needed work. Those were all things that I could fix. The game had been an excellent opportunity to see the girls in action, and it was clear that we had above-average potential. It puzzled me how girls with great soccer instincts had such poor skills. I suspected they were weak because previously, when they were on a coed team, the coaches played to win, and the boys got all the attention. That was behind us, and our all-girls team was improving. We just needed more time.

There were highlights during the game that hinted at our potential. One was a moment of personal growth elicited by a mistake. Our goalkeeper, Molly, flubbed a save. She misjudged the path of a high, bouncing ball and failed to catch it but succeeded in knocking it to the ground. Bouncing balls like that slowed time. They traveled up, paused in the air for what seemed an eternity, then began their inevitable return to the ground. Everyone observed Molly's awkward struggle as she was caught out of position. Before she could scoop up the ball, the other team kicked it into the goal. Molly was embarrassed. She retrieved the ball and then started to cry uncontrollably.

"Uh-oh," Coach Emily said in a forbidding tone.

I asked, "Is she going to be all right?"

Emily's response was not encouraging. I imagined the worst, a flustered Molly losing composure and becoming paralyzed with emotion as she stood in front of the goal, red-faced with tears streaming. I looked to our bench at Kate, who was a Turtle and a goalkeeper.

"Kate, grab your gear and check in for Molly at keeper," I said.

She jumped up, slipped on a goalkeeper jersey, and located her gloves. We were lucky. An opportunity to substitute came quickly, and a sobbing Molly came off the field to our sideline. I called her over to talk and waited for her to calm down.

With Coach Emily on my left, I glimpsed to my right at Molly.

"Are you okay?" I asked.

"Yes," she said, wiping away tears.

I paused and evaluated how to react. If I asked Molly to return to her post and she wasn't ready, she would likely melt down, the tears would return, and she might never play keeper again. On the other hand, if she took my offer as a vote of confidence in her ability, it was a teachable moment. It was tempting to do nothing and let her rest on the sideline, but then the event might have lingered in her thoughts, leading to indecision or even the yips. I tried to dispel her anxiety by saying, "Being a goalkeeper is a hard job, but we need you there. You must learn to take it in stride when the other team gets a goal. It is not your fault. If the other team scores, they defeated all seven of your teammates before they got to you, so do your best and stay composed."

Molly listened intently.

I looked at her again. "Okay?"

She silently nodded yes.

"Can you go back?" I asked.

Her expression was a mix of surprise and concern as she realized I wasn't letting her off the hook but offering the opportunity to return. She managed a shaky "Yes."

"Get a drink and check in when you are ready," I said, observing her reaction.

She glimpsed at me, then looked away, and her demeanor changed. Molly took a breath and straightened her posture, and the uncertain, sobbing girl grew calm and determined. For a moment, I felt the bond teachers experience when a struggling student has a breakthrough, but unlike an educator, I didn't teach a novel principle. I taught resilience.

Molly returned to the game immediately, looking composed as she ran onto the field to finish her shift. I suspected my assistant was jealous because it was the type of interaction usually reserved for parent and child (twist).

OUR NEXT PRACTICE was good because player tendencies began to emerge—we had cement trucks, sedans, and Porsches. Cement trucks had their dads' genes. They were tall and big-boned, characteristics that probably made them feel awkward around boys but provided an advantage under certain circumstances. One girl, Amanda, played like a cement truck with no brakes. Both her parents played college basketball. When Amanda moved with the ball, challengers bounced off. She didn't shove them down: she won every challenge with constant motion and momentum. Four of the Turtles—Kate, Megan, Marge, and Paige—were sedans. They could play anywhere, in any weather, without fail. The Porsches were Alexa, Mary, and Lucy, all amazingly fast and some high maintenance. They allowed us to move the ball quickly and catch the other team off guard. Most remarkable was that every girl on the team did something well, and none was especially weak. Accomplishing that mixture without intentionally selecting players was either a fantastic stroke of luck or weak players had been filtered out by B-team attrition.

Later that day, as we walked off the field after practice, I shared my assessment with Coach Emily. I was excited and told her we had talented players who didn't play well together because they hadn't practiced enough last year (twist). That was the last straw. I had twisted the knife once too often. Emily couldn't stand it any longer and angrily contended that the team had practiced regularly, and she had been their coach. Her anger caught me off guard. I blushed in embarrassment and apologized, but as I watched her storm off to the parking lot, it was clear that forgiveness would not be forthcoming, and no bridge would spring from those smoldering ashes. It was time to start another search for an assistant coach.

Chapter 61

Team United

W E WON OUR next game, and as the season progressed, we improved and began to jell into a team.
By the third game, many of the fundamentals of soccer had
been introduced, our defense was getting better, and I was
ready to teach something new: pushing—again. I taught it
using the same method that I used for Wade's team, but the
girls reacted differently than the boys. As I described how to
push, I could see a transformation in some players. In real
time, I saw a change in facial expressions as the realization
flowed through their brains that I was encouraging them to
push another girl physically.

Getting pushed had been a problem in some practices and
games. One of our Porsches, Mary, easily fell when pushed
and always ended up in a sobbing heap. Mary was competitive but needed training in mental toughness. Familiarizing
her with the technique of pushing was the first lesson. I explained to the girls that getting pushed was part of soccer. It
wasn't an affront, but it was intentional. If they got pushed,
they were doing something right, close to the action, and they
had to fight to stay on their feet. I don't think it had ever occurred to Mary that she should fight to stay on her feet. That

was why she fell so easily. She let herself be pushed down. As I lectured, I looked at the girls and was surprised by what I saw because they were laser focused. All eyes were on me, intensely interested. We practiced pushing for a while and then moved on, but I did not know the beast I had released until the next game.

Eliza, one of our cement trucks, quickly became the best pusher on the team. She was a solid defender and liked to play stopper. Ten minutes into our next game, she went shoulder-to-shoulder with a girl who had a breakaway. Eliza met her opponent at midfield, but the girl was fast and got a step or two ahead. Eliza pursued, made contact with her shoulder, and the contest was essentially over. The girl fought to control the ball while Eliza pushed her off the field in an arcing path that ended when the ball crossed the sideline. The ball was ours, and Eliza took the throw-in. When I enthusiastically approached to congratulate her at halftime, her first impression was that I was angry. A relieved smile burst on her face when, instead of berating her, I grabbed her hand and shook it vigorously while exclaiming what a great job she did. The entire team witnessed the exchange and watched her fear transform into gratification. From then on, they all began to push harder.

THE DEPARTURE OF my assistant coach created a vacancy that needed to be filled, so I sent a note home asking for someone else to help. I got a mom who didn't know about soccer and couldn't kick a ball well, but she was easygoing, and I could work with that. During practices, she assisted with shooting drills by rolling balls and working with goalkeepers. Her participation lasted for a couple of weeks, then she missed practice for an appointment and didn't return. At that point, I stopped trying to fill the assistant coach spot because I wasn't a stranger anymore. The parents had gotten to know me, and the determined bunch of girls I was coaching were not five years old. I thought I had been approved, so I didn't fight it. I was okay with not having an assistant for practices, but I needed help during games because unexpected things happened: injuries, hopelessly knotted shoestrings, and bruised egos. So, I contemplated who would be attending games, could handle problems, and wouldn't be insulted by my demeanor. *Hmmm.* For the second time in our relationship, Judy said "Yes," and we began a new adventure together.

NEAR THE END of the season, we played a team that became our archrival for the next four years. Our games were always close. We traded wins frequently and often tied. Their coach was tall, about 6'4", and the first time we played, he wore a white patch on his left eye. The girls called this one-eyed giant the Scary Guy. He had a booming voice and yelled at the referee almost constantly. He especially yelled at student referees who were thirteen or fourteen years old. I disapproved of that behavior; I thought he was deliberately intimidating to gain an unfair advantage. If the weather was sunny, he wore oversized mirror aviator sunglasses and no shoes. He was the only coach I encountered who warmed up a team barefooted. The girls were right; it was scary to see a tall, loud coach with mirror eyes and enormous, untanned, white feet roaming the sideline during a game. But the Scary

Guy knew soccer. His warm-up drills were fast-paced, and his goalkeepers were well-prepared. I copied everything I could from him.

WE FINISHED THE season with a winning record and a cookout organized by parents. For the most part, my relationship with the United parents was distant. We lived in neighboring villages, but civic pride made the distance that separated us feel farther than the actual three miles. Still, I welcomed the cookout; it was a great way to finish the fall season, and I appreciated the gesture, which seemed to say they were grateful.

THE SUCCESS OF our first season together fueled a fantastic spring soccer achievement. After thirteen years of attending meetings, carrying gear bags, tying shoestrings, offering tissues for runny noses, scouring the sideline for lost jewelry, teaching and reteaching skills, shuttling players, tolerating parents, cajoling players through frozen early spring practices, losing games, and winning games, my elusive coach dream, the almost impossible, unattainable dream of dreams came true. We went undefeated! We didn't go untied, but we didn't have a loss, and that was good enough for me.

Our final victory that season was an away game against the Scary Guy's team. Everything hung in the balance against his well-coached and capable team—win the game, undefeated; lose, the elusive dream lived on. No one dared speak of our undefeated status going into the game, but the girls were ready to play. We took an early lead and never relinquished it. With ten minutes remaining in the second half, Paige sealed our fate in a good way. She ripped off a line-drive ground ball that found its way into the net and put us up 3-1. What remained of the game was one of the most enjoyable ten minutes of my soccer-coaching career. Afterward, we celebrated with a few pictures, Sunny-D, and Twinkies. However, we needed something more, so I suggested stopping for ice cream at a mom-and-pop shop on the way home. It was a quiet little store in an unincorporated wide spot in the road where they sold sandwiches and ice cream to bicyclists and hikers using the nearby state forest. We shattered their peaceful afternoon with our mob of chattering girls and parents with deep pockets. I gave Paige an ice cream and a hug. She had been with Megan and me from the beginning and was always a second-half player who never quit. I couldn't describe the elation I felt when she scored that third goal, and I was grateful.

Chapter 62

Year 14–Attitude

O N A COLD, windy day the following fall, we lost our first game of the season. We were dismantled by a crack team we hadn't seen before. I didn't expect to go a second season undefeated, so when we lost, I shook it off.

"At least we got that monkey off our back," I told the girls.

I meant what I said, but I was frustrated with some girls because they disregarded my instructions during the game. I warned them not to crowd throw-ins because our competitors grew stronger every year and could throw the ball farther. Nothing I said mattered. I watched helplessly while our players took positions too close to the throwers, and the ball was catapulted over them toward the goal. I wasn't sure what to make of the disappointing performance.

They did other unusual things that fall, too. On two occasions, a group of players arrived on time but loitered in the parking lot until the warm-up phase of practice was over, then ran down to join the team as if they had just arrived. They might have gotten away with the deception had they been smart enough to conceal their presence. Instead, they warmed up on their own while the rest of the team moved on. I didn't know if their disobedience was a phase or if they needed to be reminded how easily a game could be lost. Megan confided that some United girls were unusually cliquey. They excluded her and her Turtle teammates and ridiculed me behind my back by poking fun at the surprisingly symmetrical emerging bald spot on top of my head or mimicking how I walked.

Some girls seemed to be losing interest, which I took personally because it meant my practices were tedious. I tried to rekindle their enthusiasm with something that had been a great success with Wade's team—the Jungle Run. It was a different location, but I identified a similar route. I planned to dribble through open ground, leave the balls behind, run a circuitous path over and around obstacles in the woods, retrieve the balls, and return to our practice field. We had several girls who were budding long-distance runners. I hoped that their enthusiasm would be contagious, but I was wrong. Players moaned when I introduced the idea and slumped their shoulders, saying, "Do we have to?"

I bubbled with excitement. "C'mon, it'll be fun. Something different." Then, I turned and led the way. I should have done a better job of reading the room because the run was a total bust. Even our runners hated it. There was a moment when I feared mutiny as I waited nervously for the team to emerge from the woods. Fortunately, they did return, although they were hot and grumpy. Some of them probably enjoyed the exercise and would have run through stinging nettles if I had asked them, but they were drowned out, and I continued my quest to make practices fun.

WEEKS AFTER OUR first loss, we were surprised by the Blues, a team we usually defeated. Spearheading the Blues was a girl we hadn't seen before. She was tall and physically more mature than everyone else on the field. The Blues' soccer club had a reputation for mixing players between teams to be more competitive, so I was suspicious that perhaps she wasn't enrolled on the team. However, the referee was allowing her participation, and I didn't see any point in challenging his decision. As the game unfolded, it became clear that the tall girl was special. She had outstanding footwork, and her long legs made her fast. She scored three goals quickly in the first half before the opposing coach moved her back to defense.

At halftime, I urged the team, saying, "We can beat a one-player squad because she won't be able to keep up that pace." We chipped away at the lead during the second half but fell short at the end, losing by a goal. I made a mental note that we needed to plan for the tall girl in the future. I was confident we could shut her down the next time we played.

We ended the season with two losses, and I was satisfied. What bothered me was that despite our success, I was getting attitude from a few United girls. They frustrated me because I always made a special effort to make practices fun and teach new skills, but a smoldering snottiness was infiltrating the team. I caught disdainful glances coupled with whispers, non-compliance, and tardiness. Most of it stemmed from one problem player.

OVER THE YEARS, I encountered several problem players. They all destroyed morale and divided teams. Their bad
behavior ranged from subtle, even trivial, like short-cutting
corners when they were supposed to run around them, to incredibly self-centered. On one occasion, we practiced a set
play for a corner kick. The plan was to create a clear lane for
the ball to penetrate deep to the goal, but because the problem player knew the ball's path, they intercepted it. After two
attempts, I interrupted the drill and reiterated the objective,
but the disruptive behavior didn't change, and the entire team
suffered because we were prevented from rehearsing the play.

Problem players had common characteristics. First, they
had a natural ability like speed, strength, or quickness that
gave them a standout advantage over others so that they could
achieve on their own. Second, they were lucky—with a knack
for succeeding at critical moments when a single goal or play
made them a star. Third, they didn't work to improve but relied on their natural ability; consequently, they often embarrassed themselves because of inconsistency. Lastly, problem
players almost always acted on their behalf and were unwilling to be team players.

Some coaches actively recruited problem players because of their natural ability. Those coaches prioritized winning above all else and fostered the attitude that practicing
was unnecessary. They gave players the impression that they
would get their chance to play, no matter their conduct.

I was patient. I tried to get problem players to comply
with how I expected teammates to act. I treated them like
adults and made logical appeals, explaining what we were
trying to accomplish. But there was never a magical Disney
moment when they saw the light and became team players.

It was astonishing how one rotten egg out of fifteen could disrupt practices and suck the fun out of rec soccer. Many of their teammates shared my frustration but were silent. Those teammates had to tolerate the same misconduct for years at soccer and school; they knew there was little they could do to foster change, so they patiently waited for me to give up in exasperation and move on. Their resignation was the higher path, an example of expedition behavior that good teammates employ to overcome obstacles by being tolerant and avoiding unnecessary conflict. Their silence was right, but it was not rewarded because problem players interpreted their tolerance as approval.

Problem behavior was a tough challenge because I lacked the experience and knowledge to deal with it. I was concerned that it would return in the spring, and I consulted Megan and Judy for ideas, but they had nothing new to offer. Fortunately, the season was over, and I had the winter to figure out what to do.

THE TRADITIONAL WINTER diet in our region was tough on soccer players. Cheese, sausage, brat, cookie, pizza, cheese-and-sausage sandwich. It took a toll on the girls. Every spring, I saw the extra pounds and felt their pain as they struggled to do what had been routine just a few months earlier. It wasn't their fault; it was their biology manifested in a culture that favored fatty foods and a climate that interfered with outdoor activity. Megan and a few others participated in basketball during the winter. That helped keep them in shape until the snow melted and the ground thawed.

That spring, my intuition was correct: some girls showed up with big butts and big attitudes. A contributing factor was that I wasn't the new, fun coach anymore. Instead, I was the familiar coach who liked discipline and hard work. Not all the girls were a problem; many were great, but the in-group/out-group dynamic made the team irritable. I ignored the drama and pushed through the fog of hostility with fast-paced practices that replaced in-fighting with intense activity and shortness of breath. That solution felt a little like denial, but I was a soccer coach, not a psychologist, and I didn't think there was anything I could have said that would have changed their behaviors. It was a power struggle, and my strategy was to avoid playing by their rules—instead of using words, I made them work at soccer practice. If things had gone wrong, that solution could have produced more angst, but all that soccer activity made us play well enough to win our first two games, and morale improved. Success became contagious, and the girls got back into the groove of practices and playing together as a team.

OUR THIRD GAME was against the Blues, and we formulated a plan to counteract their star player. Our strategy was to plaster a capable player on her as often as possible. That player was Alexa, one of our team's most gifted and gracious. I knew she didn't want the job because it was demanding; she would be in the spotlight, and if she failed, everyone would know. To reduce the pressure on Alexa, the team and I discussed her role and agreed that everyone had to bring their A-game if she was willing to take on the challenge.

On game day, our team showed up on time and focused. We had a good warm-up and a solid starting line-up. The only thing missing was the Blues' star player; she was nowhere to be found.

Our well-primed team took about one minute to score the first goal. I looked at Judy and said, "Oh, that was fast." Another minute—another goal, and I began to realize what I had done. The other team kicked off, and we intercepted—another goal. Three goals in three minutes—I had created a monster and unleashed it on the Blues. I spent the previous week firing the girls up for the game; unfortunately, the team we prepared for lacked its star player, and the remaining Blues were unprepared for us. Eight minutes into the contest, I readied the first batch of substitute players and established an *ad hoc* rule.

"Anyone who had bagged a goal couldn't shoot again but was permitted to aid teammates who hadn't scored."

I intended to slow our pace, but the girls interpreted the meaning of the rule differently. They thought I was encouraging them to identify every player who hadn't scored and facilitate their success. The rule slowed our scoring rate slightly but encouraged more passing, making our team more difficult to defend. More goals ensued.

At halftime, I modified the rule, "Anyone who had scored a goal couldn't shoot again, *and* every player on our team had to touch the ball before a shot could be taken," or "Intentionally kick the ball to their goalkeeper." After years of being trained to kick the ball into the goal instinctively, the girls found the latter alternative difficult, so they embraced the former, and an extraordinary demonstration followed. The restriction that every player had to touch the ball did not go unheeded. They were all alert and communicating while constantly moving to open spaces. That awareness and positioning facilitated our passing game, but the outcome was incredibly confusing to the Blues because our objective was unpredictable. We weren't moving toward the goal. We had a different agenda emphasizing passing so every player could touch the ball. It was a whirling, twirling, passing tornado—a Passnado.

The Passnado decelerated our attack, but the other team was hopelessly defeated. I felt sympathy for the Blues. It was unusual for us to dominate so thoroughly, and it was the first occasion when I was the coach of a murderous, heartless scoring machine that crushed our opponent's spirit. I tried to stop it, but the girls were so amped up at the beginning of the game that when they slowed down, the Blues didn't have the strength to put together a scoring attack. At least we didn't talk trash, and they didn't have to suffer Losers' Walk.

Chapter 63

Burnout

PHYSICAL PAIN WAS part of coaching. I did what I could to stay fit: I ran occasionally, walked frequently, and participated in soccer practice when a player needed a partner or to show the team that I was willing to do what I asked of them. But every year, my soccer pain intensified. Kicking the ball twisted my lower back, and quick stops hurt my knees. My day job contributed as well. I was on my feet all day at work and developed a nasty case of plantar fasciitis in my right foot. The doctor who diagnosed it told me the inflammation was treatable and prescribed $600 orthotic insoles which were absolutely the most uncomfortable things I ever walked on. They didn't help. As our soccer season progressed to its end, I was suffering. I was tired of the pain and disgusted by players with bad attitudes.

In addition, I seemed surrounded by teams with coaches who had played soccer and knew the game better than me. I tried to learn from them but felt like I was always playing catch-up. It was impossible to observe their coaching, borrow what they did well, and avoid a feeling of inferiority. I knew that my efforts to learn the game of soccer made me a good coach, but I wasn't great because I lacked the experience that comes from playing the game, and no amount of study could correct that weakness.

OUR LAST GAME that spring was a good one. We played shorthanded and came back from a two-point deficit to tie. I was proud of that comeback. The girls kept fighting, but it bothered me that four players didn't attend the game. I wondered if maybe I was taking my role too seriously. After that, I didn't do anything except think for weeks. Then, I made the biggest mistake of my coaching career. It was a pain- and frustration-induced call for help, written to the new club president, Coach Janet, the soccer zealot who spoke at the coaches' meeting. I offered to step aside if someone with more experience was interested in coaching. I advocated for a coach with more experience than me who knew what they were doing. I knew there were people like that around because I competed against them frequently. Maybe someone was waiting for an opportunity to coach a team. That couldn't happen unless I were willing to step aside and create an opening.

I was naive and doomed to relearn that not everyone shared my coaching philosophy. No experienced coach was available, and I was not consulted. What followed was either an act of cronyism, laziness, or desperation. The outcome wasn't good and confirmed my previous experience: the only thing more difficult than training my child's soccer team was enduring a bad coach training my child's soccer team.

Chapter 64

Year 15–Worst Fear Realized

T HAT FALL, WITHOUT a word from the Soccer Club, I was replaced by another parent, Coach Stan. The team advanced to U13 status and the big field, 11v11. Coach Stan's daughter, Jenna, was a year older than the girls on Megan's team and the only remaining member of the U14 team. The League allowed U13 and U14 players to be combined, so Jenna, the oldest, took charge.

At the first practice, I dropped Megan off, introduced myself to Coach Stan, and offered to help. He shook my hand and glared at me without saying a word. There was a long, awkward pause. Then, after a moment or two, I stopped smiling and deduced that his silence was my answer—he didn't want my help, and the cold stare was his way of telling me to get lost.

THE FOLLOWING WEEKS were confusing and frustrating for Megan because Coach Stan attended practices and games, but he let Jenna do the coaching. He shouldn't have. Jenna made decisions based on what she wanted rather than what was best for the team. She gave herself the starring role and made her friend, who was the only problem player on Megan's team, co-star. Week after week, without regard for skill or success, Jenna put herself and her friend at center forward, a position that offered great potential to score goals. She didn't understand that center forwards didn't get an opportunity unless someone passed them the ball. The team was so disorganized that they couldn't manage it. She bullied two of the Turtles and routinely assigned other girls to positions inconsistent with their natural abilities. Morale plummeted, and attendance at practices declined. The team was soundly defeated frequently and went two seasons, fall and spring, without a victory. It was a dark time.

Megan never missed a practice or a game, but her mood suffered from a sense of powerlessness because practices weren't fun, games were poorly managed, and there was no hope that things would change. I felt as if I had abandoned my daughter and the rest of the team, and I second-guessed how I had asked for help. I attended games from the parents' side of the field and watched the dysfunction. The teamwork I had worked to build was gone, and individual strengths were ignored. The only thing I could do was chauffeur Megan and some other girls when they needed rides and purchase ice cream after embarrassing losses.

I tried to stay in touch with players by encouraging them when they made smart decisions on the field; however, I was careful to avoid confusion about who was coaching the team. Consequently, I managed to maintain a thread of connection with some of the girls, who seemed grateful for the interaction. I was relieved that they didn't harbor any animosity. More than once, when the time was right, I tried to inspire by paraphrasing the nineteenth-century German philosopher Friedrich Nietzsche, "What doesn't kill you makes you stronger." The response was always the same: a shaky smile, an aspect of determination, and surprise that I knew the lyrics to a familiar Kelly Clarkson song.

Chapter 65

Year 16–Back in the Saddle

TWO GOOD THINGS happened during my yearlong hiatus from coaching. The first was that my health improved. My back recovered, my knees stopped aching, and I went to a different podiatrist who prescribed a treatment plan that was almost free: take a handful of ibuprofen three times a day and perform calf stretches using the bottom step of a stairway. Three weeks later, I was cured after years of pain.

The second good thing was that with Jenna's graduation from the team, I could return as coach. I contacted the club and informed them I was interested in the job. They granted my request. Weeks later, I was back at the coaches' meeting at the park pavilion, listening to a soccer zealot lecture. Coach Janet lectured us to stay off the fields. She briefed us on how frequently the club received compliments from other teams about the high-quality turf at the complex. The club wanted to maintain that standard, so she encouraged the group to stay off the fields. I was puzzled by her statement and looked around at the coaches who shared my table; no one made eye contact, and there was no hint that they shared my confusion. I wondered if they had heard it before and were doodling away their indignation.

I wanted to interject, "Soccer fields are not made to grow grass," but I fought the urge and kept my mouth shut like the other coaches. I wouldn't have been upset if she had encouraged us to stay off the lines. That was ingrained in me during my high school football days when coaches awarded push-ups to players who committed the infraction of rubbing paint off a line by mindlessly standing on it. Volunteers like me painted the lines on soccer fields. It was a thankless, invisible job that required time and attention to detail to do well, and I appreciated that effort. Consequently, I routinely avoided using lines during soccer practices.

I also avoided using the goals when the ground was soft. Don't use the fields? The entire soccer complex was covered with fields! Where did she think we were going to practice? There is a reason why teams don't play on lineless fields. I learned that fact during my first soccer experience with Owen when I resorted to using toilet paper to construct a kickoff line. From my perspective, it made no sense to forego team success for the vanity of having a showcase facility because goalkeepers need to practice in goals, penalty-box drills need a penalty box, and soccer fields are not made to grow grass—they're made for playing soccer.

When the coaches' meeting concluded, Janet took me aside. Most of the girls on the team were in eighth grade; the following year, they would be at the high school. Consequently, Coach Janet took a unique interest. She wanted to know if she could run a skills clinic during our usual practice. I agreed it would be great and suggested that the girls could benefit from some work with moves to escape with the ball. Those techniques were a weakness because I had never played soccer and didn't know how to teach them. We set the date.

The other thing she told me was that the club was sponsoring a professional soccer camp during the weeks leading up to rec soccer and paying a premium to have one of the coaches stay on for several weeks in the fall to circulate among teams. She wanted to know if I was willing to participate. I was astonished. It was exactly what I asked for when I wrote my letter to the club—find an experienced coach for the team! I confirmed I would gladly accept all the help I could get.

ALMOST EVERY PLAYER on the team welcomed the return to a familiar normal under my supervision. Players who atrophied under the previous coach found new vigor. The snottiness was gone, and if it dared rear its head, a teammate chopped it off; they had no patience for it because they were glad to be back in what felt like a winning groove.

The soccer camp coach's name was Ethan. He was in his early twenties, fit, charismatic, and had a British accent. No girl wanted to disappoint him. He played a crucial role in revitalizing the team. His practices were like mine. He didn't make players run but conducted fast-paced drills that involved running. No one suggested his purpose was to educate coaches, but I used the opportunity to learn from someone knowledgeable. Ethan was easygoing, informative, and welcomed my participation. Our team practiced twice weekly; Ethan took Tuesdays from start to finish, teaching soccer skills. On those days, I fell back into my old role of assistant, chasing stray soccer balls and doing anything to keep practice moving: if a player needed a partner, I filled in; if Ethan wanted to work with goalkeepers, I took the rest of the crew. I had the team to myself on Thursdays when I mimicked his warm-up and then worked on team play. A great 50/50 mix of clinics and group practices prepared us for the first game.

I THOUGHT THAT our first game was going to be a test. I was uncertain how much damage Jenna's influence caused. Under her regime, the team had dissolved into individuals and hadn't played cooperative soccer in a year. Some girls had lost interest in playing. When I received the roster at the start of the season and saw who was missing from the team, I contacted lost players and asked if they wanted to return. Then, I called the club registrar and begged to facilitate late registration. They all came back. I did it because I knew the girls who quit and why. I knew they loved playing soccer but had been driven away by unfair treatment. I didn't want their soccer experience and my history with them to end that way; however, I was concerned about the aftereffects of bullying and favoritism. I thought most of the girls had put those things behind them and subscribed to Ethan's work ethic and my emphasis on pursuing a common goal.

If my intuition were wrong, the same way it was about the Jungle Run, it would be a long fall soccer season.

IN THEIR FIRST game, Team United faced an opponent that soundly defeated them twice during the previous year. I put our best lineup on the field, where everyone started in their comfort position and contributed—win or lose, we were doing it together. The scheme had worked before, and I hoped it would again. The teams seemed equally matched initially, but a new winning attitude revealed itself as the game unfolded, probably catching the other team off guard. Our sturdy defenders tirelessly fought off attackers, robbed them of the ball, and passed it to the sides where our Porsches anxiously waited, like horses at a starting gate, bucking off any opponent that tried to mark them. When the pass came, those speedy girls blasted down the sideline, closely followed across the field by forwards and midfielders who knew to push up but avoid being offside. Then, the Porsches bent their run to the goal or passed the ball to a waiting teammate across the field. Our flexible, cooperative approach involved everyone, and it succeeded.

Hard-kicked balls rebounded off defenders and the goalkeeper. Some of them found the back of the net. We won the game 2-1. Coach Stan, who had rebuffed my offer of assistance during the dismal previous year, attended the game on the parents' sideline. He didn't speak to me, but his presence made the game's outcome a twofold victory—a win for the team and a twinge of satisfaction from payback for his cold stare.

Chapter 66

Do As I Say, Not As I Do

THE FOLLOWING WEEK, Coach Janet's clinic was confusing and awkward. She was the same soccer zealot who had rebuked coaches for holding practices on soccer fields, but she didn't hesitate to use them for her clinic, and even worse, her first action was to tell the girls to fall in on the painted sideline.

As she commanded the girls, she walked past me and made eye contact as if to question if I noticed the lack of compliance with her own rules. I didn't say a word, but my body language probably conveyed the message. She looked guilty, as if caught red-handed doing something she knew was wrong.

We used the field and lines for the duration of the "clinic," which was more of a title than a workout—Coach Janet seemed unprepared. After a brief warm-up, she spaced out several cones on a sideline and then a second opposing line of cones about five yards from the first. It was the soccer-move part of the clinic that I had encouraged. Moves were necessary because when one of our players with the ball met a defender, they needed a technique to escape. Unfortunately, I never played soccer, so my ability to teach escape moves was basic.

There are many soccer moves named after players who invented them. They range from simple feints like a head-fake to complex multi-step maneuvers. Coach Janet paced and barked orders as the girls lined up behind the cones, "Dribble to the cone, make a move, then dribble back. I want to see Maradonas, Cruyffs, scissors, and Rabonas. Let's go."

The girls just stood awkwardly, not knowing what to do. Had it been a cartoon, there would have been the sound of screeching tires and a car crash. None of them knew what any of those names meant.

I responded in a businesslike fashion because I didn't want to seem disrespectful during a potentially embarrassing moment.

"They don't know how to do those moves," I said.

Coach Janet paused for a moment, then demonstrated a Maradona while describing her actions aloud, "Dribble to the cone, stop the ball's forward motion by tapping it with your right foot, hop over the ball while spinning and drag it with your left foot, then dribble back to the line."

It was a complicated sequence of actions—not my first choice for a clinic on introductory soccer moves—but the girls followed instructions and began taking turns. I observed and tried to help players who were struggling. After a few minutes, a question that begged an answer occurred to me: *How does one use the move to escape a defender?*

So, I asked Coach Janet, "What's the context for this move? Where is the defender positioned?"

Her response was brusque, "First, the technique, the context can come later."

Feeling frustrated at her refusal to answer an obvious question, I understood her meaning: she wanted me to butt out. I stopped trying to help, stood back, watched, and listened, hoping to learn something. Unfortunately, neither the players nor I acquired any new soccer moves that day.

What should have happened was a progression, where the introduction of the Maradona was made more realistic by adding a constrained defender so players could dribble toward an opponent and execute the move, but she didn't do that. Instead, we practiced a potentially valuable technique but had no idea how to employ it. As a result, no player ever had the confidence to attempt a Maradona during one of our games.

WHAT FRUSTRATED ME about Coach Janet was her hypocrisy. She preached, "Stay off the fields and lines," but used them herself; she lectured coaches about practices but was unprepared at her clinic; and she emphasized teaching but refused to answer my questions. There were other things as well. One especially bothered me because she thought she was doing the right thing.

At the high school, when Coach Janet knew that her team would play a much weaker opponent, she encouraged her players to achieve a score differential of at least ten points by halftime to invoke the slaughter rule and end the game. I think she was trying to motivate players to work even though their adversary wasn't challenging, but what did she expect them to learn from crushing an overpowered opponent? She was behaving like the Purples. Her goal was to win the league, and the less-capable teams encountered on the way to that objective were nothing more than sparring partners.

I objected to Coach Janet's approach because her behavior disrespected others. She should have achieved a score differential sufficient to ensure the outcome, then used the opportunity to increase the experience of future players by letting second-stringers take the field. That would have benefited her team while allowing the opposing team to finish the game against an opponent whose ability was more commensurate with their own.

I understood Coach Janet's effort to motivate her team, but I thought her method was wrong. My coaching experience was limited, but one rec soccer interaction guided my thoughts. Once, during a game when we were soundly defeating a weaker opponent, Lucy, one of our most competitive players, stood beside me and remarked, "It's too easy. It's not fun." She could score almost at will but felt no reward because the contest wasn't challenging. Scoring didn't make her a better player, it just demoralized the other team, and she knew their pain. If a twelve-year-old could understand that aspect of a game, a high school coach should too.

Chapter 67

Megan's Aha Moment

A̲S WEEKS WENT by, we racked up more wins. Megan emerged as a confident, quiet leader, but she wasn't the only one: Alexa, Amanda, and Marge were all rocks of leadership, too. Megan's development was extraordinary because I witnessed one instant when something clicked for her, like flipping a switch, and there was an immediate change in behavior.

It happened midseason, when practices could become tedious because a routine was established, but the last game seemed far off. We were halfway through one of Ethan's trainings when he called for a water break. The sweltering afternoon sun had exhausted Megan; she dragged to the sideline and sat with Amanda. When Ethan called the team back to the practice field, Megan and Amanda lingered while the others quickly complied.

Their behavior disappointed me because Ethan's call to return was not negotiable. He expected them to obey, and I thought they were being disrespectful. As the two girls slowly rolled off their butts and started to get up, I looked at them, and they at me.

"Don't be last," was all I said.

For some reason, my words struck a nerve. Both players jumped, far more motivated than thirteen-year-old girls usually were when I goaded them. Perhaps they were motivated because my suggestion was a relatively attainable goal—they didn't need to be first, they just had to avoid being last. Or maybe since they were both literally last, my comment prompted competition. Whatever the cause, from that moment on, Megan took more of an active leadership role and was almost always first. Much of her success was driven by her powerful legs, which gave her an advantage, and she became the *de facto* corner kicker. The calculus was simple for her and the team: they needed someone with a solid leg to execute corner kicks, and she could do it consistently. Consequently, she got the job. There was never a contest for the position. Other girls didn't want it because they lacked strength or ability. Success bred confidence for Megan and the team.

I wasn't in charge of practice that day; I was a spare part, a human cone, but my words spoken at the right time strongly affected Megan's development. Being part of her transformation from diminutive outsider to leader was one of the best accomplishments of my life.

Chapter 68

Challenging Conditions Produce
a Great Effort

THAT FALL, WE played a game that became my proud-
est day as coach of Megan's team. I tried to reschedule
it to accommodate several players who could not attend but
failed when the opposing coach would not return my calls.
The situation was frustrating because the opposing coach was
the Scary Guy. I had rescheduled games at his request, but he
refused to reciprocate. If he intended to achieve an advantage,
he succeeded—the day was a scorcher, with temperatures in
the mid-nineties, and we had only twelve players, leaving
one surplus player for substitutions. With only one sub, many
girls would be on the field for an entire half, enduring twenty-five minutes of strenuous activity without a break.

We warmed up and prepared for a challenging contest as
game time approached. It was hot, but we had practiced on
comparable days, so the girls were uncomfortable but physically acclimated to the heat. About five minutes before game
time, I assembled the team and explained what I thought was
coming. I told them I had tried rescheduling the game, but the
other coach would not return my calls. I also told them the

other team planned to take advantage of our low numbers and exhaust us. That got their attention; then, I tried to be positive.

"Play our game and make good passes and traps, so we don't waste energy chasing balls. Put your hand up if you get hurt or thirsty, and I will sub you as soon as I can."

Nobody said anything. They just listened and took a last drink. Then I extended my arm and made a fist.

"Everybody in."

They stacked their hands on top of mine, and we did our traditional cheer before I listed off player positions and sent them onto the pitch. With everyone where they belonged, I looked at Judy and our one extra player.

"Here we go."

The Scary Guy's eyes had morphed from mirror to metallic blue, but everything else was the same. He bellowed at the referee, and his squad was well-trained. The game was close. His team pushed hard at first, but our defense was solid. I substituted my one player frequently, and we seemed to be doing well except for Lucy, who absolutely hated to lose. As the game unfolded, we fell behind. The effect of the temperature compounded Lucy's frustration with the score, and she lost her composure midway through the first half. She didn't abandon her position but stood on the field crying, her face contorted with emotion, and with her hand up to signal that she needed attention. I substituted, and she came off the field wailing, "I quit, I quit, I quit, I quit." She was one of our best players but had been completely rattled—it was the only time I saw her that way.

As she stood beside me, sobbing uncontrollably and shouting, "I quit; I don't want to play anymore," I considered options. I remembered what Coach Dan had done all those years ago with that little boy who was intimidated and wanted to sit out.

Give her what she wants, I thought.

"Okay," I said firmly and clearly.

The effect on Lucy was immediate. Like that little boy, I could see in her face the realization that she had just taken herself out of a game that she loved to play.

"Go sit down and get some water," I told her.

She went, and I worried we would have to finish the game without substitutes if she didn't bounce back. I didn't need to worry for long since the trick worked. Lucy was at my side two minutes later, begging to return to the game. I let her rest for a few minutes, then sent her back to play the rest of the game without a problem.

When the whistle blew at halftime, our opponent led 2-1. We were in the game but feeling the effects of the heat. Judy and I spent halftime refilling water bottles and dowsing players over the head. Fortunately, a patch of shade was nearby, so we moved away from the field and camped there. There was little talk as girls sprawled in the shade, disgruntled, feeling like the conditions were unfair.

About one minute into halftime, the Scary Guy sent his players back onto the field. They took up their positions and waited. I couldn't believe it. *What a jerk*, I thought. The halftime interval was five minutes. Sometimes, coaches agreed to cut halftime short to get a game over quickly. Usually, the circumstances involved playing in a freezing downpour or extreme cold and windy conditions. That day was different. He was baiting us, trying to get us to forego our only water break. When I saw what was happening, I resolved not to be manipulated and turned my back to the field. I told the girls that the

Scary Guy was trying to rush us back to take advantage of our low number, but we weren't going for it. No one objected. We used halftime to get watered and recharged, letting the other team stand on the field and roast.

The referee blew his whistle a few minutes later, calling us back. A solemn bunch of girls took their spots on the field. We played well. The Scary Guy was in his usual form, constantly yelling at the referee until something happened midway through the half. We were pressuring hard near his goal. The more we pressured, the more the Scary Guy roared, and then Paige blasted a hard shot from near the top of the penalty box. The line-drive ball rose from the ground as it rocketed toward an empty corner of the net about shoulder high, but it never made it. One of the opposing players, not the goalkeeper, stuck her arm straight out and interrupted the ball's trajectory. She was tall, skinny, and looked like a one-armed utility pole with her arm fully extended. The ball hit her in the wrist, then fell to the ground, and the goalkeeper quickly snatched it up. It was an intentional and obvious infraction. Only the goalkeeper could use their hands or arms to control the ball. As I watched the keeper recover the ball, I waited for the whistle, but it never came. There were uniformed referees on the sidelines and on the field who should have made the call. Finally, I couldn't contain myself and decided that if the refs blatantly favored the home team, I would call them out.

"Handball—in the box!" I shouted.

Nothing changed on the field; however, the Scary Guy immediately stopped yelling at the ref because the enormous gift was more than he hoped to achieve. A handball inside the penalty box was supposed to result in a penalty kick, but neither the referee nor the linesmen, one of whom was the local

Soccer Club's president and a soccer zealot, saw it that way. I didn't complain further. The game was ongoing, and there was no point in distracting my team with theatrics—it was the right decision. Despite the biased refs, we battled back and tied the game a few minutes later.

When the final whistle blew, the score was 2-2, and I was proud. We shook hands and then moved back to our space on the sideline. The team was drenched in sweat, dehydrated, and exhausted. Most girls lined up single file, desperate for more water from Judy, who dispensed it from a large jug. I checked on injuries and then turned to look at all of them. I had to say something to recognize how hard they played. I knew some were disappointed that we did not win, especially with the handball, which should have been the deciding goal.

So, I said, "Hey," to get their attention and waited for them to look at me. "They can tie us, but they can't beat us," I beamed. "I am so proud of how you played today—short-handed in this heat. Great job."

Then I went around shaking hands and congratulating every one of them. Teenage girls are hard to read. I couldn't tell if they understood what I was trying to convey. They were so drained that they just wanted to go home. I think some of them knew. I hope so—they played a great game.

THERE WERE ALWAYS a couple of teams in the mix that were better coached and had better skills than us, teams that probably played indoor soccer during winter and tournaments during the summer. Those teams were an eye-opening challenge, a reminder that someone was better no matter how good we were. Nevertheless, it was a fun time. The girls were happy to be playing up to their potential and winning again. Megan noticed a change in attitude after the dark time with Jenna. Previously, she had been excluded, and I was the subject of ridicule; afterward, we were respected for what we contributed.

Andy's Advice ... on Decorum for Coaches and Parents

Recreational soccer is for the benefit of players, not coaches or fans.

For coaches:

1. **Keep it fun:** As teams progress and the competition intensifies, it's important to remember that recreational soccer is meant to be fun and educational. Strive to maintain high performance standards but avoid being overly competitive.
2. **Be fair** with your opponent: When unsure what action to take, imagine yourself in your opponent's shoes and remember your team is watching. What you do will be a model for their behavior in the future.
3. **Don't reprimand every player** for an infraction committed by one. Collective punishment gives the problem player power over everyone else and causes discord on the team.
4. **Go high:** Resist the temptation to sink to the level of an opponent with low standards of sportsmanship. Stick to your game plan.
5. **Keep your cool:** If you need to report inappropriate behavior during a game, wait until halftime or the end to inform the referee. Don't start a shouting match during the game.

For parents:

1. **Soccer can be a rough sport.** Your child will be involved in physical acts like pushing and collisions. Those acts are an unavoidable part of the game and should be taken in a spirit of competition and without anger.
2. **Leave cowbells and the twelfth man at home.** Disruptive behaviors don't belong at recreational games where the goal is fun, fitness, and education.
3. **Don't take referee inconsistency too seriously.** The rigor of enforcement of the game's laws changes as players advance. Most referees have the best intentions.

4. **Don't demean the coach in front of your player.** Players may have a good relationship with the coach, and your comments will be offensive.
5. **Keep some perspective:** Don't bring a tournament attitude to a recreational soccer game. Adjust your expectations for the circumstances.

Chapter 69

'I Think I Just Killed Mr. Beers'

IN THE SPRING, team United assembled for a last gratifying season. Our final practice was unforgettable, especially for me. The Gator Day tradition made it feel like a national holiday. Tart bottles of citrus-flavored sugar water were my way of rewarding the squad for consistent attendance and hard work. I intended the day to be a fun, player's-choice day, but with me regulating to prevent it from degrading into a bunch of girls standing around talking.

Practice started well. The girls had great attitudes, and we progressed through several minigames. With thirty minutes to go, I tried something new. I selected a goalkeeper and established two lines at midfield with the players facing the goal. Then I stood between the lines, slightly behind the first players so they couldn't see me. When everyone was ready, with eyes forward (looking back was cheating), I kicked the ball toward the goal, and the first two girls in each line charged after it, competing for control and an opportunity to shoot. The drill worked well; everyone was running, it was challenging, and the keeper was getting some 1v1 practice. All good. But eventually, the running began to wear them down. I expected that. It meant they were getting a workout.

I wanted them to work a while longer, so when Paige toed the starting line without a partner because everybody else was gassed, I volunteered.

"I'll go," I said, and I stepped in.

Instantly, there was a sense of excitement in the air. I glanced at Paige. She smiled back, looking embarrassed but willing. Everyone else watched the impending contest.

"Somebody kick the ball," I instructed, and I turned to face the goal.

Time seemed to slow. The world fell silent, and I was aware of a slight chill in the evening air. The stillness was broken by the sound of a foot on a ball, and I saw my target shoot away and curve toward Paige's line of attack. From my ready position, I pushed hard off my right foot. I felt the leather of my shoe stretch under the force, and a grunt escaped my lips as I put everything I had into getting a quick start. One, two, three steps in, I was neck and neck with Paige, who was probably not trying as hard as me. We jostled together, and she eased up, perhaps because she felt like a kid on a bicycle going head-to-head with a locomotive. I got a step on her, took control of the ball, and tapped in an easy goal with my left foot. I turned back to the lines, disappointed that she had not challenged me more, and joked, "Anybody else want to go?"

Marge turned and raised her hand, "I will."

As I jogged back to the beginning of the line, Marge's nickname should have given me pause—we called her Marge the Destroyer. The name was our inside joke. Marge tended to collide with goalkeepers. A more accurate moniker would have been Marge the Tenacious. She was one of our go-to players who earned the name because she never quit. She was two-footed, as good with her left foot as with her right. That was not something I taught her: it was a natural ability. Goalkeeper after goalkeeper fell victim to Marge's ease with the ball. If she got the ball one-on-one with a goalkeeper, she dribbled straight at the doomed individual. At some point, the keeper committed to an attack, and no matter which foot the ball was on, Marge shifted the ball away and finessed it into the goal.

The danger was that Marge's approach brought her close to goalkeepers. When they misjudged the ball's position because of Marge's quickness, only her feet and legs remained. Then, there was a collision and a smack of flesh on flesh. With the keeper at Marge's feet, momentum carried her upper body forward, and she tumbled, often in spectacular head-over-heels fashion.

Marge never got a yellow card; she didn't mean to cause injury. Her play was how soccer was intended—don't stop until the goalkeeper has control. The aftermath was always confusing when Marge and the keeper were down, and parents cried out in alarm. Judy would gasp and utter, "Oh no," as the ball rolled to a stop in the goal, and someone on our sideline would say, "She's done it again." The injuries were minor, but a tentative goalkeeper was in for a long day if Marge was hot. Somehow, she always escaped unscathed. I should have remembered that on our last day of practice, but I got caught up in fun.

As Marge and I teed up for another start, a fever was in the air. All the girls began lining up; everyone wanted a piece of the action. I didn't know how I was going to run against all of them, but I was willing to try.

I liked Marge. She was a well-behaved girl who had been

with the team for years. She had four siblings who made time management an issue for her parents. One of their solutions was to drop Marge off an hour early for practice; consequently, when Megan and I arrived to set up, Marge was there, desperate for attention, bursting with pent-up energy and unleashing a babbling tumult describing her day. She talked so rapidly that I could only catch the gist of her breathless monologues and nod in agreement at what seemed like appropriate times.

As we waited for the ball to be kicked, there was no threat in the challenge. We were just friends playing. I don't think she or I cared who won. I would have been pleased if Marge embarrassed me with a signature move, but the game never got that far.

I was ready at the thud of the ball. It was a fair start, and the ball went evenly between Marge and me. I exploded from the starting line as before, keeping pace with her. Our bodies got closer as we approached the ball, bumping shoulders. She laughed, and I gained a half step.

I'm ahead again, I thought, surprised. I hadn't expected to be ahead. Close enough now, I touched the ball with my left foot, redirecting it away from Marge and toward the goal, but my touch was too strong. The ball shot farther ahead than I intended, so I lengthened my stride to make up the difference. I pushed hard off my right foot, then down on my left. Halfway through the powerful step, I felt something snap. There was no sound, but my brain perceived a low, long vibration, like a cracking knuckle, except it was in my left thigh. I felt the pop, then tissue pulled free and moved under my skin. Part of it went toward my knee; part went toward my hip. The pain was about a four out of ten.

I coasted to a stop, limping, before leaning over with hands on knees. The goalkeeper scooped up the rolling ball, and Marge peeled off, saying, "I think I just killed Mr. Beers."

Someone asked if I was all right. I didn't answer. I didn't know. I hobbled off the field so the drill could continue, but the girls were finished with it. My absence was noted as I took a knee and tried to assess the damage. Megan asked if I was okay. The realization that I was hurt was starting to sink in, and I motioned to her, waffling my hand back and forth as if to say, "So-so." Then, not too concerned, she asked if they could practice corner kicks. I agreed that was a great idea, so the girls practiced independently for ten minutes before convening in a circle in front of the goal to chat. At that point, everyone was done with practice, and I began collecting soccer balls and equipment. The girls helped me carry the equipment to the truck, then we all went our separate ways.

My day ended in the emergency room. After a quick assessment, the doctor told me that I had a strain with minor tearing of the quadriceps muscle in my leg. No surgery was needed—my leg would heal on its own. That was good news, but I wished I had held back a little. It was a quiet ride home from the hospital. Judy did the driving and remarked that it was ironic that I made it through all those years of coaching without injury and got hurt at the last practice. But, in retrospect, it wasn't ironic. It was predictable. The girls were faster, and I was older than ever but playing like a teenager. If there was going to be an injury, that was the likely day.

Chapter 70

Graduation

THREE DAYS LATER, I limped around a university campus, watching my oldest child, Owen, graduate from college. The boy who started it all had completed a degree in biochemistry and was enrolled in graduate school to continue his education. It struck me as odd that Owen's graduation happened simultaneously with Megan's and my farewell to rec soccer. Both events marked the beginning of a time of change for our family. Things would be different as Owen prepared for his new life a thousand miles away. He would move out of our home and probably never move back. I felt more strongly about that than I did about the conclusion of rec soccer and Megan's transition to high school. It made me wonder if I had done the right thing. I gave up a lot to coach my kids' soccer teams. Without that responsibility every weekend of every spring and fall, there would have been more fishing and camping trips—more shared experiences. But because of our choices, the Beers family had traded those activities for soccer's version of adventure, and there was no going back.

There was no doubt that Owen was ready to fledge. He was intelligent, determined, confident, and a little too big for our household. Some of those characteristics had their roots in his soccer history. So, as I shifted my aching leg on the drive home, I asked myself, *Was it worth it? Would I do it again?*

Chapter 71

Last Day Together

MEGAN'S LAST RECREATIONAL league soccer game was rained out, which was disappointing. There was interest in rescheduling, but it wasn't easy late in the season, so our final official match slipped away. The parents of Megan's team were not like the parents of Wade's. Except for the barbecue at the end of our first season, they didn't give coach gifts or cookie parties, so nobody planned an end-of-the-season celebration. Instead, we played our last games together and said goodbye at a Memorial Day weekend tournament—three games in one day with a chance to win our division.

The weather was perfect for soccer—high overcast, dry, and cool. Yet, we failed to sweep the tournament when we lost our second game to a more aggressive team from a bigger soccer program. Our team took it in stride. They had learned that expecting to win every game wasn't realistic. Instead, we enjoyed a beautiful spring day, had fun, and were happy winning two of three games. For us, the tournament was free of controversy. It was a good end.

Chapter 72

Owen Moves Out

IN EARLY AUGUST, Owen packed his things for graduate school. It was a time of turmoil. Judy and I were anxious because Owen was starting a life that was truly his own. He had a new vehicle, apartment, and state residency. Previously, he had lived within three hours of home and frequently visited on weekends, so we saw him several times a year. Unfortunately, his next move was too far for a weekend visit. We knew we would only see him at Christmas and for a week during summer. The rest was uncertain.

Owen was nervous as he attempted to get everything he needed into his truck and a 5x9 U-Haul trailer. He laid out the load in our basement, then in our living room as the departure day approached. Like Judy and me, Owen had misgivings about the move—we were a close family, and he was moving away from that. As he packed up, Judy and I encouraged him to organize the remaining stuff in his room into collections to be kept and discarded. His room hadn't been repainted in thirteen years, and we knew it needed updating.

I went to his room the day after he left to see what remained. I expected to find several piles that required hours to process, but Owen had embraced the task with uncharacteristic efficiency. Almost nothing remained. There were only a few items on the walls: a postcard from the Grand Canyon, a cross-stitched plaque made for him by his aunt, and some soccer team photos. Those things meant something, but the books, posters, toys, and knickknacks that boys collect were gone, and so was the essence of Owen.

For a moment, I was stunned by the realization that my role as a parent had changed—that I had gone through that threshold unaware. From the day he was born, I nurtured and encouraged him to work hard and be smart so that he would be self-sufficient. Then he grew up and did it. I felt regret. I stood there with tears streaming down my face, angry that he had moved out so thoroughly. I knew he had not taken all his things, and I couldn't believe he had thrown so much in the trash.

After a while, I regained my composure. I looked at the soccer pictures. There were three spanning third grade to high school. Then I turned and looked at the rest of the room. Only an empty bed and bookshelves remained—except for the closet. I held out hope and opened the door. It also contained empty shelves, bare hangers, and belongings that were not Owen's. One of those things was a large basket in the bottom left side of the closet. I picked it up and examined its insignificant contents. Then, I noticed a plastic storage container underneath the basket. I removed the white lid and found the possessions I searched for—favorite books, models, toys, awards, and several small trophies. They were not tournament trophies, but rec soccer trophies that were given as a concrete way to recognize his effort and reinforce the idea that working hard and having a good attitude was right, even if his team did not win every game.

Soccer zealots said the trophies were meaningless, but they meant a great deal to Owen. He had saved them for thirteen years and then saved them again in that plastic tub with all his favorite things. I looked at the team names listed on each trophy and wondered how often I called them to assemble players or encourage: Sabers, Bullet Dogs, Rhinos, and Rockies. Something about holding objects from that time helped me remember, and I wondered if that was why Owen saved them. A flood of faces and events came rushing back, but no final scores came to mind. Those outcomes, once so important, weren't worth remembering.

Chapter 73

Megan's Evolution

EARLIER THAT SPRING, during practice, one of the girls on Megan's team asked what I thought of their chances in high school. I told them they would have a good team if they stayed together. Unfortunately, they didn't—competing sports and life drew them apart. Soccer, track, and tennis were all spring sports for girls in high school. Participating on multiple teams was impossible, so some had to make tough choices. Girls who lived in different school districts made the short drive to play with the rec United team, but they didn't have plans to change school districts for soccer. Some just grew tired of soccer and moved on to other things.

Megan stuck with it, and her soccer-facilitated transformation into a leader continued. She did not have great endurance, but she was a determined defender, and her strong leg made her stand out enough that she succeeded in making the varsity squad as a freshman along with Lucy. As a sophomore, Megan continued to be a solid player, for which she was rewarded with more playing time. By the time she was a junior, her ability had grown, but some strong seniors were ahead of her. Megan contributed a supporting role, relishing every occasion to play. They had a good team and made a run at winning their conference tournament but were defeated in the semifinal round.

That year, Coach Janet resigned, and her assistant, Roman, took over the team. He was well-liked, and the team flourished. As a senior, Megan stepped in to fill a void in leadership. In contrast, the team's leading scorer was demanding and temperamental. She screamed at her teammates routinely when they made a mistake, and when the error was hers, she blamed others. Always critical and negative, she tore down the team. Megan counteracted the drama by acting as a stabilizing influence, encouraging teammates, directing the defense, and taking corner kicks and free kicks. For a second year in a row, the team made a run at the conference championship but was eliminated in the semi, plagued by injuries at key positions.

FOR ME, THE highlight of Megan's last soccer season was not her team's run at the conference championship but a brief event that demonstrated what she learned during years of soccer activity. It came near the end of a playoff game against an opponent who had defeated Megan's team earlier in the season. On that occasion, Megan's crew was short of personnel. Out of desperation, Coach Roman moved Megan from her usual defender position to forward. The change was a major misjudgment. Neither Coach Roman nor I understood how important Megan was to their defense. The other team scored three easy goals in the first half before Roman countered their attack by moving Megan back to her usual position. It was a different story for the playoffs. Megan's team had its full complement, and she was in command of the defense.

The game was away at a soccer complex that felt compact. The bleachers were unusually close to the pitch, and the crowd was loud, spearheaded by obnoxious male students. They jeered Megan's teammates positioned near them. The game took a turn when our team fought off an attack and had a breakaway. Our midfielder charged down the sideline with the ball. She crossed the center line and was met by a sprinting defender intent on stopping the attack. The two competitors collided in the last third of the field with a solid thwack as the defender shouldered Megan's teammate to the ground. The deliberate take-down was an infraction, and the referee awarded a direct free kick. Seconds elapsed while the two teams prepared: the grounded players jumped up and moved closer to the goal, the defense pushed up, and Megan stepped in to take the kick. The boys in the stands roared at Megan as players jostled for position before the goal. My daughter took a few seconds to evaluate what was before her.

The spot of the foul was far enough from the goal that everyone assumed Megan would put the ball into play. While her teammates milled around trying to create open space, the keeper stepped away from the net, intent on catching the ball before it reached the ground. Megan saw an opening—the keeper's advance left the far side of the goal uncovered. Megan signaled she was ready, stepped to the ball, and blasted a hard line drive. The ball rocketed over the heads of every player on the field, including the goalkeeper. It found the far corner of the net, and our bleachers erupted with cheers and applause; the boisterous boys were silenced for the rest of the game.

Megan jogged forward, propelled by momentum into a mob of ecstatic teammates. Her goal was a heartbreaker for the other team and cemented the win. It was an amazing moment that no one expected.

"I can't believe she did that," spilled from my mouth, and Judy agreed. It was another of those life thresholds that I didn't see coming; Megan wasn't my *little* daughter anymore. No more stuffed animals, Care Bears, or asthma struggles. She was the decisive leader of a soccer team.

Chapter 74

Honors for Megan

LATER THAT SUMMER, Megan's team had its soccer banquet. Coach Roman encouraged Judy and me to attend because "There will be some honors." His statement was vague—there were always honors at an awards banquet; I assumed he meant the usual varsity letters, etc.

The banquet was a potluck at a player's house. Megan joined her friends when we arrived, and Judy and I mingled. It was out of character for me, but the event was one soccer meeting that I didn't mind attending. Three girls from the United team were seniors, and I wanted to congratulate them one last time. The awards started after dinner. The junior varsity coach presented first, acknowledging player participation. Then, Coach Roman recognized team managers and varsity players. The process took a while because each girl received a few words, a handshake, and a round of applause.

Next on the agenda were all-conference honors. Those were players nominated by coaches as best-in-conference, then voted on by all coaches. Megan was awarded first-team honors. When I heard her name, I was proud. She had worn the captain's armband all season, but best-in-conference was taking it to a level I hadn't anticipated. After that, Roman awarded the most valuable player to the leading scorer on the team.

At that point, I thought the event was over, and I was delighted with its outcome, but Roman continued. One more award, the Mia Hamm Award for team leadership—was presented to Megan! I was amazed when he announced her name. My brain responded as it had when she scored her last goal: first disbelief, then "Wow." I was proud, proud, proud. I don't know why I was surprised. I should have anticipated the award because Roman celebrated many of the same qualities that I observed when she played on the rec team: confidence, leading by example, and supporting teammates during challenging times. Afterward, I enthusiastically hugged her while declaring her achievement a great accomplishment. Then I thanked Roman, congratulated the other girls, and we put soccer behind us.

Chapter 75

Synthesis

DURING MY TIME as a coach, my competitive record ranged from a low of guiding a committed and hard-working group of boys to a scoreless and winless season, to a high of leading a talented and determined team of girls to an undefeated record. The breadth of experience gave me perspective.

Life is not fair, and neither is soccer. We try to make it fair but only manage to impose rules and restrict each team to the same number of players on the field—and sometimes, we fail even at that. Soccer is unfair because humans are not machines; they are not all the same, and player ability varies. Teams win because they have an unfair advantage: a midfielder with large lung capacity and incredible endurance, a forward with above-average fast-twitch muscle and explosive speed, or a tall goalkeeper. Soccer is not like bowling, where players in a handicap league can win if they have a better-than-average personal best day. That's why emphasizing winning above all in recreational sports is wrong, and the idea that trophies are only for tournaments is flawed.

The contrasting argument is that recognition should be given to players who deserve it, not to players who happen to be on the team that won the game. Who should be more respected: the outstanding player on a losing team, or a reserve player on a winning team who never set foot on the field? In a competitive world, people want to know who is best in the league, the nation, and the world. However, rec soccer for seven-year-old children should have a different emphasis because the outcomes of their games are unimportant. They don't decide championships or generate points that increase rank. Who wins becomes insignificant after the final whistle because the motivation for the experience is to teach the game, play, and have fun.

Megan never received a trophy. Her soccer experience began after the Beers Trophy Incident and medallion-awarding soccer banquets. Instead, we awarded T-shirts. She didn't seem worse for wear by the substitution, suggesting that what matters is why an award is given rather than what is given. When we awarded trophies or T-shirts, we didn't advertise the event or have a banquet. We had a simple ceremony where I recognized each player for their effort and congratulated them with an adult handshake. The message was the same regardless of the award: showing up and working hard is not easy, but it leads to improvement and positive personal growth. That message only resonates if individuals with more life experience, like parents and coaches, take the time to highlight it. It's an act of leadership that goes with raising a child.

TOO MUCH COMPETITION brings out the worst in human beings. It leads to a slippery slope where competitive spirit snowballs into cheating. Faced with conflicts of interest like fame and money, intense competitors often gradually forego the virtues of sportsmanship and begin a descent into unsportsmanlike conduct that is reinforced with every success. That's why world-class athletes deflate footballs to throw more accurately and dope blood to ride bicycles faster. Our solutions to preventing those behaviors are imperfect; eliminating scorekeeping is not the answer. Still, something is wrong when coaches, referees, and players routinely manipulate the outcome of games to achieve victory. When the rules are skirted or ignored, the game is no longer fair and becomes frustratingly pointless. That's not what recreational sports should be.

There is an unwritten rule in soccer that provides a way to pause a game when an injury occurs. I never received the courtesy, but I did confer it on an opposing team when one of their players lay on the ground crying in pain, grasping a knee. It was heartbreaking to see a child suffer under those circumstances, but referees are trained to overlook such incidents and to allow play to continue until it is interrupted by the natural flow of the game. The injured player was close to our sideline, and we had the ball nearby. When I realized the ref would not immediately stop the action, I firmly instructed my advancing player to kick the ball off the field.

"Pass the ball to me," I shouted.

The confused player paused, and I reiterated the order.

"Pass the ball to me now!"

The player complied, and as the ball rolled off the field at my feet, the referee blew the whistle, pausing the game. The opposing coach thanked me as he ran onto the field to attend to his injured player.

Not once did I see that unwritten rule demonstrated by

any other recreational or high school team during my time coaching. In every instance where it could have been employed, opponents continued or intensified their attacks. They all perceived an injured opponent as an opportunity to achieve an advantage. That attitude illustrated that something was missing—sportsmanship.

Sportsmanship is defined in many ways; most definitions emphasize respect for an opponent, fairness, and graciousness in winning or losing. Some also include the intrinsic reward of participating for the joy of playing. A lack of sportsmanship was the root of many negative interactions I experienced. It infiltrated everything, including league meetings, club soccer boards, officials, coaches, parents, and ultimately, players. What replaced it was a focus on winning; consequently, there was plenty of advice about other celebrated aspects of soccer like high standards of achievement, fitness, growing the game, innovation, collaboration, enthusiasm, confidence building, and leadership development. The mission statement pages of many soccer organizations echo these same values without mentioning sportsmanship, though they do touch on some aspects of it. If they include sportsmanship information, it is often uncategorized and can only be uncovered after drilling down through layers of content. Since the topic is rarely emphasized and difficult to find, it is not surprising that many soccer enthusiasts need to be made aware of appropriate behavior. Essential characteristics of sportsmanship include[1]:

- Honor the game. It's a privilege to be associated with the sport of soccer, so behave accordingly.

---

1 J. C. Harves, "The Unwritten Rules of Soccer," CoachingAmericanSoccer.com, 2024, https://coachingamericansoccer.com/soccer-rules/the-unwritten-rules-of-soccer/.

- Respect teammates, coaches, managers, and everyone associated with your team. Most are trying to do their best.
- Respect the opponent. Without them, there would be no game.
- Respect the referees. Without them, there would be no order.
- Respect the fans. Most spectators appreciate a well-played match.
- Play fair. Do not intentionally injure opponents; abide by the game's laws and their spirit and intent.
- Don't inflate the score. Unnecessary scoring against a weaker opponent is inappropriate.
- No demeaning celebrations. A brief act of exuberance by a player or team after scoring a goal or a win is reasonable but should not demean an opponent.
- Lend a hand. Assist a player who has fallen to the ground; offer a hand to help them back to their feet.
- Intentionally put the ball out of play upon serious injury. Serious injuries require immediate attention.
- No racism. Racism is unacceptable.
- No trash-talking. Let your play speak for itself.
- Shake hands. Honor your opponent, the game, and yourself with a sincere handshake.

THE GOAL-SEEKING BEHAVIOR innate in humans pits us against each other. We compete for scarce resources like money, food, and soccer victories. The methods we use to obtain those resources range from self-serving to altruistic.

Human biology rewards both behaviors with the same chemical chain reaction in our brains. So, choosing the right path is difficult, especially for inexperienced individuals.

Soccer is a competitive sport. How we compete when playing soccer depends on what is encouraged by the individuals in leadership positions. State soccer associations, referees, club presidents, coaches, parents, and team captains all bear some responsibility. The hierarchy in place provides a mechanism for communicating what's expected and appropriate behavior.

Leadership is the key to encouraging the correct level of competitiveness. Leaders can inspire players to crush an opponent and revel in their destruction, or strive for a personal best performance and extend the hand of sportsmanship in gratitude for a well-played game. Both approaches have merits and weaknesses; the correct one depends on the situation.

Competition in sports can be viewed as a continuum. Recreational soccer lies at the left end of the spectrum, where young players are first introduced to the sport. Fun and sportsmanship should be emphasized over winning and game scores. Players should be encouraged to play all positions, and playing time should be equally distributed as long as attendance requirements and effort expectations are met. As players advance in experience to the center of the spectrum, the emphasis at practices should shift from developing individual skills to fostering teamwork and a big-picture game perspective. Encouraging respect for teammates and opponents during this stage helps build trust and empathy. These attributes of sportsmanship have relevance beyond rec sports and should be reinforced as players transition to more competitive select (club) teams and high school, which are at the competitive end of the spectrum.

The win/loss record is appropriately the standard by which club and high school teams are judged. But a team's record of achievement for a season pales compared to the importance of lessons learned by its players. For most athletes, recreational and high school activities are the only opportunities to participate in competitive sports. What they learn stays with them and sets the tone for coaching interactions in the future. When they learn to embarrass a weaker opponent by inflicting a slaughter-rule-inducing lopsided victory by halftime, future coaches will likely repeat the behavior because experience has taught them it is appropriate, and the cycle repeats. Missteps like this can be avoided if coaches and players imagine themselves in their opponent's shoes and question if a better alternative exists.

The urge to compete is ingrained in human nature. For most people, there is something more rewarding about a competitive victory than a personal victory. That tendency might someday be superseded by the idea that participating in a sport is its reward, but until that time, the best way for children and adults to compete in sports is to strive for a win and then be honest and ask, "At what cost was success achieved? Was anyone hurt because of unsportsmanlike conduct? Was an opponent humiliated? Were the rules broken to achieve an unfair advantage?" A person who competes and considers those things recognizes that competition can be corrupted if it isn't fair and can correct their actions in the future. That way, when players shake hands at the end of the game, they can genuinely say, "Good game."

Chapter 76

Would I Do It Again?

WOULD I DO it again? I gave up a lot to coach soccer for my children, but it was often difficult to tell if the sacrifice was worth the reward. I often wondered, *Did I make the right decision and do what was best?* Parenting is about making choices. The catch is that you seldom know if your decisions are correct. In each instance, you choose a path based on an assessment of the current situation and what you think will be best for your child. Then you watch and see what happens.

The sixteen years when I coached were grueling and rewarding. They included some of the worst and best moments of my life. I was thirty-six when I started coaching and fifty-two when I stopped. Much of the experience flew by because the pace of my life was fast, but there were occasions when time seemed to slow down. Those were moments when I witnessed fantastic events that were so incredible that my brain burned the sights and sounds into memory—my daughter's last goal, Wade's first goal, and Owen's flashes of brilliance.

I often joked that soccer was my other job because I worked at my daytime occupation and then came home to my parental soccer side hustle. Both were productive: one provided money to live on, and the other provided currency for a rewarding life. The best thing about my family's soccer odyssey was not reflected by events like goals or flashes of brilliance on the field; those were memorable but not life changing. The most rewarding aspect of soccer was how it changed my children. Soccer made all of them physically fit. It taught them that if they worked, they could accomplish spectacular achievements. It allowed Owen to form strong friendships with his teammates and experience the success that comes with teamwork. It helped Wade build physical strength and mental confidence. Megan's transformation was truly amazing, and all my kids became better leaders.

Chilly Saturday mornings and dewy grass often evoke a nostalgic longing for my soccer coaching days. When I ask myself what I miss, I conclude that it is not the game but the players who became my friends. Most of them have gone their separate ways, and I will never see them again. However, some are still around, and I encounter them occasionally. When I do, we share a handshake and, I hope, a certain level of trust that comes from having struggled and succeeded together. As for my three players, they are going on with their lives. I see the boys less often now that they have graduated from college, but I see Megan every few weeks. When she is home, I still try to get a hug every night before she goes off to her room. My life as a soccer coach made my children better people and brought our family together, and along the way, we witnessed some spectacular moments that I will never forget. Would I do it again? Absolutely.

Epilogue

A RECURRING THEME IN this book is that parents routinely make decisions without knowing the correct course of action. Judy and I had those concerns, but now I can reflect on the outcome of the choices we made while coaching and parenting. There was so much more than soccer. Our special efforts began when our children were two years old. Judy encouraged our children to cultivate a few close friendships outside our family. As they grew older, we required our children to do chores like cleaning their rooms. We limited video game play and urged them to play outdoors and participate in athletics. We began encouraging them to work outside our home at about twelve years old; the boys did lawn service, and Megan babysat. We spent hours on homework when they needed help and gave them autonomy when they didn't. We encouraged them to ask teachers for help, especially in math and science. They all graduated high school and college. Owen earned a master's degree and is a technical expert for an engineering firm. Wade graduated with a Ph.D. and is employed doing medical research. Megan is a middle-school science teacher. They all have driver's licenses and live independently. I am unsure what metric to use to judge a successful life, but I think we gave them a good start.

Acknowledgments

I AM DEEPLY GRATEFUL to my amazing wife for her soccer assistance and steadfast support in this project. She proves again and again that accomplishing difficult things is easier with the help of a true friend.

I thank my children for allowing me to be part of their soccer lives. I cherish the experiences that we shared and look forward to many more.

I am grateful to Kris R., my literary lifeline, for encouragement and for plowing through an early draft that was embarrassingly rough. I am also indebted to my friend John H. for his honest and professional feedback that improved the manuscript. And to my soccer buddy Jay B., thank you for your enthusiasm. There were occasions when I second-guessed the merit of this project. Your support helped make the dream a reality.

I am profoundly grateful to my players and their parents. The hard work, gift certificates, cookies, and moral support gave me the confidence to continue.

Lastly, I thank those who read this book, contemplate the message, and choose to become part of the solution. Your efforts may go unacknowledged, but they will make a better experience for the children you encounter.

About the Author

A NDY BEERS IS a father, husband, avid outdoorsman, and always on the lookout to apply the skills he acquired while earning a Ph.D. in environmental science. Andy was twice awarded Coach of the Year by his hometown club and has enjoyed numerous mementos, gift certificates, cookies, and cakes from grateful players and parents. As a youth soccer coach who is between jobs, Andy bides his time until his next adventure on the pitch by traveling with his family, pursuing an ongoing dispute with a vintage outboard motor, and contemplating why things are the way they are. Although Andy can't claim the status of a professional athlete, the problem-solving skills that he mastered as a research scientist have helped him logically evaluate how factors that limit the success of typical children and adults can be overcome or used to their advantage. Andy's method has been successful over a broad range of applications, including coaching, parenting, research, and manufacturing. Applying critical thinking to youth soccer helped Andy identify positive outcomes regardless of whether matches were won or lost and allowed him to teach strategies for success in life beyond the game.

For more information and to contact the author, visit www.andy-beers.com.